BLACK MAN ISLAND

LARRY J PERODIN

Book contains profanity, racial epithets and subject matter that may not be suitable for children under the age of 18.

Copyright © 2020 Larry J Perodin

All rights reserved.

Published by Future Now, LLC 2020

Dedication

Dedicated to our Black ancestors, ex slaves. To give voices to those who had a voice but could not speak. They had to watch what they said. Watch how they spoke. When they spoke. Who they spoke to.

They had to watch themselves at all times. Not in a mirror but through the eyes of white people always eying them. Watch where they went. When they went. Who they went with. How they looked no matter where they went. How they acted when they went.

If our Black ancestors sat up in their graves, looked about, what would they have to say, about the state of affairs in the Black Community. Looking back at what they went through, would they be happy, sad, turnover in their graves? What would they say to Black America?

If our Black ancestors could finally quench the fire so long, 'shut up in their bones,' say a word or two. If they could finally exercise their first amendment rights of free speech. Say what's really on their minds. What would they say to white America?

Contents

PREFACE

Our addiction is not our affliction America.

Many of the problems of Black America are nothing more than symptoms of a lethal cancer that is spreading. America looks the other way, maybe the problems will go away? Maybe America prays, "patient heal thyself."

The problems of Black on Black crime, scant Black Healthcare, failing schools, high Black unemployment, discrimination in lending practices against Blacks, etc. etc., are symptoms of a raging sickness threatening to consume not just Black America but all America.

America is still in a Civil War, with slight adjustments. The north supposedly won the war. But that war was like fighting with your little brother. After you beat him, you made up immediately afterwards. Seems America then turned its anger to who, what started the war. Slavery and Black people, the what and who that came in between the brothers.

Seems Blacks in America are on their own, still fighting to get off the plantation, fighting for equality, fairness, fighting for fractions of an inch America begrudgingly is unwilling to give.

Today in America, politicians glowingly talk of the booming economy, the rising stock market, appreciating home values but if the financial boats of all Black folk are not rising, then what good is that?

If we plant seeds of positivity in a few children but do nothing for our struggling Black children, what good is that? If we free the young, gifted and Black child, but do nothing for those not so gifted, what good is that?

If we create schools that are the shining examples of what all schools should look like but there is no plan to make all public schools in the Black community as such, what good is that?

If we don't pay off all college student loans, what have we done by paying off a few? If all college debt is paid off but we don't ensure all Black kids are equipped with bankable skills, what good is that?

If we revitalize certain neighborhoods and leave all the Black neighborhoods to fester and rot away, what good is that? They become a place that no one wants and what have we allowed to happen?

If all boats don't rise together in 'The Land of Opportunity,' 'Land of the Free, Home of the Brave,' 'The Greatest Nation Ever,' what good is that? Is it okay that all the others are lost, sink to the bottom? Is it a numbers game? We can't save everyone, so we write off the expendable, specifically Black people, left behind, struggling on this new plantation.

Introduction

This f'd up picture

I'm sitting here trying to figure this out. But I'm unable to. Nothing seems to add up. Not with all the talent, all the resources at our disposal, it doesn't make sense. The answers elude me. I'm left dumbfounded.

It's not easy to self-reflect, then bash oneself over the head, hard because of what you see. Faced with the truth and it does not change no matter how long you stare into the mirror. It's not a pretty picture.

I stared into the mirror, knowing full well, to look deeply into the mirror can be painful. Leading one to search his or her soul, lay oneself bare, exposed, on the operating table. Not knowing if the doctor will say, "There is nothing we can do, stich them back up. It's not worth it. The patient only has a week, maybe a month at most."

It's the question we desperately want answered, what's ailing us. But can we handle the answer, the truth, the bad news? Can we handle the news we really don't want to hear, the worse possible news?

Pressed by curiosity we peak inside this envelope. We want the answers. With exposure we open ourselves to pain, criticism. All our sins are laid bare. Fact is, the Bible says at some point we all will have to give an accounting of ourselves, to God, to mankind. Or can we go to the grave shrouded in secrecy. Hoping our family, our friends, our enemies, the world, our God, will never know the truth. Is that how it is, our deathbed hope, to hope nobody, and I do mean nobody finds out the truth about us?

I sat there thinking, then surmised something has to be done. Just get it all out. How else can problems be solved, if we don't expose the truth? Let the chips fall where they may. Of course, some feelings will be hurt, friendships lost, families split apart. There could be some fights, some people tossed into jail, lose their job.

Is it worth it? To confess, let it all out, leave nothing unexposed. Talking about oneself, about one's family, about friends, allies, about 'my people'. Can you do it? Can we take it? What will be their reaction?

If you put the truth out there, you might think the crowd running toward you is congratulatory. On the other hand, they may want you strung up or run out of town tarred and feathered. "Get out, the sooner the better" is the mob's cry. Sounds too much like that Jesus talk nobody wants to hear.

That being said, all you have to do is pick up a paper, turn on the evening news. There it is exposed, the truth about Black America. Or if you have the nerve, you can get it raw. Walk the streets of the inner city. You'll get a picture of what's really going on. An endless cycle of violence, poverty, despair and hopelessness is etched across faces.

Most of the people are in denial, believing in some ragtag politician, talking about change, a change gonna come. The youth cry out with defiance and are ignored. Still others are plain numb to what's going on. To a certain extent, seems America has become numb to what's going on. Still others really don't care. It's as if they all agree, 'this will never change', that all too familiar unwritten law. Then again, it is perhaps easier to believe it's not real, just a *Jerry Springer*, or *Cops* type reality show.

We grab hold of our drug of choice, to help numb the pain, to subdue the wave of emotions headed our way. Stare into the tv mirror, take a hit or sip of something, to soften the blow of reality. It may not be drugs or alcohol, maybe a box of chocolates. Seems most folks are blinded by the shades of their world. Most thinking, "as long as it doesn't affect me and mine, why should I care one way or another. Besides, what can I do anyway?"

Episode one, finds Black boys robbing and stealing at nine and ten. Selling dope at eleven and twelve, to eat, help mom pay bills. A hit man at fourteen, considered the best at sixteen. 'Treat them as an adult' is the cry of the people, 'they man enough to do the crime, let them do the time.' Sadly, the judicial system gladly obliges. There is no hope for them is the theme of Episodes two, on this reality tv show. They are written off before they become men. Episode three, explores the broken revolving door of the jail house Black lives are trapped in. Why? Why ask why? It's just the way it is.

In Episodes four and five, we find barely teenaged girls running barefoot and pregnant, no father in the home. Oh there's a step dad around, he may be the baby's father. The paternity test is coming at the end of the show. Then again, maybe the baby's father is dead, in jail. Maybe the father is an unknown set of possibilities? We will explore the possibilities in Episodes six and seven. At any rate, the father is AWOL, nowhere to be found. That is if we can believe the mother. Episode eight, finds our girls working a kinda prostitution. The only way to make ends meet, least till they can get on the system. The system, why that's a whole nother season.

Mothers are on welfare, and their mothers, and their mothers' mothers, all trapped by the system. And the mothers before all of them, sharecroppers and slaves. They were and are totally dependent on this plantation system indigenous to America. There is no damn freedom, no escape. Just this f'd up picture. And the people feel hopeless, can't change a damn thing.

The credits roll by and there is no need to worry, more is in store. Stay tuned for a word from our proud sponsors, then exciting and controversial scenes from next season. The gasps, the oohs and aahs have us hooked. The phone lines are lit up with calls to family and friends. We can't wait to see just how bad it can get. Who will survive? Who will make it off the plantation?

I'm sitting here listening to some Gil Scot Heron, he's talking about 'The Other Side,' his words run cold in my bones, "and it might not be better if I never went home again." Knowing full well that is the case. There is no other side. It is what it is, just this f'd up picture,

America seems to have turned into a reality show. So what's the answer, the solution? Nothing but 'fuck it,' that's it. Try and get as far away as you can. Escape as fast as you can. Never look back.

If you are fortunate to escape the inner city, most will agree, it's best you never went back home. Why should you go back, to look at what will never change? Maybe get caught up in an old beef. Maybe get caught up in an old habit with some old friends. So you face the unverified but widely accepted fact, one person can't change a damn thing. Besides there's always charity. If need be, you give at the office, tithe at the church house, pay for a funeral, to subside the guilt.

As you turn the pages of the local paper, get towards the very back. Maybe catch a glimpse of the very ending of the evening news program. You may find some good news. You'll hear and see rays of hope for the Blacks still struggling in the inner city. Little Johnny made it to the pros, took his momma with him to a new home. Little Susie finally got her big break, she's on her way to Hollywood. The smart girls and boys in the books found their way out with scholarships to college, got good paying jobs.

What we don't hear about is all the 'Little Johnnies' that didn't make it to the pros, had their bubbles burst. All the 'Little Susies' that didn't make it in Hollywood, came back used and abused. We don't hear about all the boys and girls that didn't have a support system to help them get out to college, get out to anywhere. They had no parent, no teacher, no big mamma, nobody. What are they left to do? Do we even care? It does not matter what inner city street you walk down. For the most part, this f'd up picture is what you'll find, an endless cycle of violence, despair and hopelessness etched across faces.

Everyone wants change. But no one wants the truth, the uncut truth. How can you change a damn thing if you keep lying to yourself, to each other, avoiding the mirror, refusing to accept the fact this is real and f'd up? Something must be done now. Marvin sang so prophetically about it in 1971, 'inner city blues make me wanna holler, throw up both my hands. Trigger happy policing. Panic is spreading. God knows where we heading.' It should be obvious by now, we're not heading anywhere, no time soon, unless something is done.

SLAVES & THEIR DESCENDANTS

V.

UNITED STATES OF AMERICA

Part I. The Opening Statement

THE REPARATIONS QUESTION

Why is it when the subject of reparations comes up, America goes tone deaf? It's a taboo conversation. Implying, we don't discuss that round here. You bring it up, it's as if you're having a one-sided conversation. No one is interested in responding.

Right off I must confess. I drank the Kool Aid. In my youth of the 70s, I considered myself a progressive. America was the land of opportunity. The sky was the limit. Look out for number one was my mantra. Go out into the world, take your lemons and make lemonade was my motto. Don't talk to me about how difficult things are out there in the real world. Try working harder, burning some midnight oil. And you'll make it for sure.

So if you asked me about reparations in the 70s, 80s, I was against it. I had my philosophical one-liners, I was like, "man go get a job. The post office always hiring. Maybe you gotta start at the bottom, flipping McDonald's burgers. Work your way to the top, become a minority owner. Guess what? It's been done before. You don't have to reinvent the wheel man. Just get off your ass and stop complaining."

Brother run up to me, asking can I spare a dime? Another brother on the street corner waving, trying to flag me down. No sir, sorry, I wasn't giving the brother begging one thin dime. I'll give him some free advice. "Try the post office." What do I look like helping a brother look healthier than me? Ain't nothing wrong with these brothers. To all my advice was, "man go pick up trash, mop somebody's floor." Why should I give up my hard-earned money? Brothers gotta take responsibility for their actions or inactions. That's what I believed. The Kool Aid was good.

I was coming along at the right place, at the right time in America. My ancestors had paved the way. By the 1970s the tide of history had turned in Black folk's favor. On July 2, 1964 President Lyndon Johnson signed the Civil Rights Bill. It was the most powerful civil rights legislation ever signed into law. It effectively ended segregation. All that Jim Crow stuff was over. There would be no separate bathrooms, water fountains, schools, restaurants. Employers couldn't discriminate based on race, sex. Blacks deserved better and it was high time they got it.

In 1965 President Lyndon Johnson signed an executive order on Affirmative Action. A mechanism to help right the ship of Blacks being held back, being held down for so long. This opened the door for Blacks to obtain better paying jobs. Jobs on par with whites, even though the pay was not quite the same. If you had a government contract or relied heavily on the government in your business, you were strongly encouraged to hire Blacks or give contracts to minority firms.

In 1977 congress created the minority set aside programs. Small minority businesses were given advantage when bidding on government related contracts. In the 70s Black millionaires were being made left and right, in business, entertainment, in sports. We had *Ebony* and *Jet* magazines. We had *Soul Train*, *The Jeffersons*. So why would we need reparations was my mindset.

In the 1970s being Black finally had some advantages. If you were a Black female in business, why that was a double minority advantage. If you had your shit together, you were in demand. I think that's when use of the term, 'token Black' became highly popular. Blacks were glad to oblige, if it pays the bills, who was complaining.

We were seated at the table. Blacks were appointed to prestigious boards, given management jobs, placed in positions of authority. We were wearing suits to work. We were decision makers. We were, 'moving on up.'

The 70s was our breakthrough decade. James Brown preached, 'Say It Loud, I'm Black and I'm proud'. And we were proud. The Black power movement was upon us. The 1968 Olympics helped set the tone for the 70s. My man John Carlos and Tommie Smith threw up the power sign on the winner's platform. Blacks were like, hell yeah. We don't have to take no mess no more, from nobody.

Political change was underfoot. The Jim Crow south saw a reversal of fortune for Blacks. The large Black population that remained down south were suddenly in charge. They became the majority or a significant voting bloc in many cities and voted Blacks into office.

Blacks in the densely populated cities of the north organized and created solid voting blocs. These voting blocs had political clout. The 70s saw an explosion of Blacks get elected to positions of power, to state and national offices. Black mayors were elected in major U. S. cities, Cleveland, Atlanta, Los Angeles and New Orleans.

With financial gains and political clout, Blacks began moving into traditional 'white neighborhoods,' driving fancy cars. Living just like white folks. *Good Times* was a thing of the past, *The Jefferson's* was the new reality.

Then, seemingly without warning, the 80s happened. It happened so suddenly. Blacks didn't even see it coming. Who could have predicted it? It was as if the wheels came off. After a meteoric rise, Black America began to flame out like disco. Black America began to split in two, Blacks that could figure it out and Blacks that couldn't. It was a mad scramble to get out and nothing else mattered. It was as if our souls had left us.

Our Black communities began to erode. Whites got tired of seeing Blacks move in next door. They got the hell out, quickly. Maybe Blacks thought they'd be happy to see a prosperous Black family move next door, add some color to the neighborhood. They were sorely mistaken. Whites left the inner city neighborhoods in a mass exodus, to a place called suburbia, pseudo for utopia or simply, no Blacks.

To their shock, the Blacks that could afford it followed. The pro athletes, the successful entertainers, the political elite, the business elite, the hardworking middle class, they all got the hell out. Even the successful dope dealer got the hell out, though he kept his dope house in operation.

It was no longer okay to be poor for Blacks. Once Blacks were satisfied to collect green stamps, saving for the seemingly impossible prize in the magazine. Once it was okay to collect the box of commodities, tide us over till we got back on our feet. But no more, Blacks hotly pursued that dream. Get off the plantation, in search of the elusive American Dream, that white man lifestyle.

It was a trap door. Exposing the fragileness of the Black American fabric. Not everyone had what it took to get off the plantation, to break the chains. All men are not created equal in all ways. All men are not equally strong. This opened the door to the treadmill of dependence. For many, it became easier to succumb to the plantation than get off.

By the 1980s the final nail in the coffin came. Some diabolical mind created a blockbuster dependency, 'crack cocaine.' That did it. Blacks in the inner city might not could afford cocaine but they damn sure could afford crack. Crime skyrocketed. Blacks got used to the new normal. New phrases were coined, 'Black on Black crime,' 'gang banging.' The murder rate began to skyrocket. The jail cells began to burst with Black men, creating a booming new industry, the prison system. What happened to Black pride? Gone, even James Brown succumbed to drugs and was thrown into jail. That was it. It was as if someone opened the door and tossed Black pride out.

What happened to our old neighborhoods? They became run-down ghettos. What about our old public schools? They became graffiti ridden and rat infested. And instead of learning reading, writing and arithmetic, kids were taught how to pass a test. What about mom's old church? It might still be there, but reverend moved to the suburbs. He commutes back and forth. What about Black owned businesses? Gone, like an old song once played on the radio, gone, gone, gone. And the jobs that remain are few and hard to find.

Something obviously was amiss. An awakening, this is not a reality show. The conditions of Black America's inner cities are not random. So if you ask me about reparations today, my answer is 'hell yes, we need reparations'. Inner City Black America is in free fall. Down, down, down, and hell might not look too bad. This thing is too big, too important to dress over, ignore.

There has to be more to this situation than meets the eye. Something is desperately wrong with inner city Black America. We are at top of all the wrong categories. It's unexplainable. We are sinking into the abyss and I dare say we may not be able to recover. They say the rising tide lifts all boats. Not so in Black America, the nation's economy is booming but the inner city's boats of Black America have holes in them. They are sinking. The inner cities of Black America are going nowhere, seemingly sabotaged by the government sworn to protect and serve.

In 1865 the Civil War came to an end, bringing an end to *legal slavery* but then immediately afterwards, a new war began, to maintain a slavery system. One hundred years later in 1964, 1965, Civil Rights legislation put a pause on the slavery system of Blacks in America. White America then made a tall leap. America is done with this slavery thing. Unfortunately, all the poison was not cut out of the wounds of slavery, on both sides. Thus this misguided government allowed the wounds to fester. The dirty little secret is out. The prognosis, the cancer that was in remission is back and spreading to vital organs.

Cries for help go out from Black America. The cries go ignored. Painful fires stoke up from time to time, but the fires are quickly tamped out. Yet embers are still burning. Rather than do what is necessary, the government throws fuel on the fire. Now there is a fire raging in Black America, that is threatening to consume all America, from shore to shining shore. Why is this happening? Does America want the truth, the uncut truth? Then the question must be addressed openly *with malice towards none.* Seeking only to *bind up our nation's wounds*, finally.

Whereas, The Plaintiffs hope to prove through the preponderance of evidence, that the remnants of SLAVERY IN AMERICA, are the cause of Black America's litany of problems and conditions. Further, meaningful reparations and changes in laws

are the only solution to those problems. Through the discourse of this book we hope to present said evidence to prove this case and therefore, we pray for payment of unspecified damages from these United States of America.

Part II. The Evidence

MY FEET ARE TIRED TOO!

I know the subject of reparations is controversial in America. So first off, if I offend, I apologize. No, on second thought, I take that back. I don't care who I offend. I have a saying I live by. When I listen in earnest to the problems of others, at some point I have to politely interject, 'I have to eat too.' If I can't get you to acknowledge my plight, then why should I acknowledge yours? Is it a game where we argue whose problem is bigger, whose is more important? A pissing contest, who can piss the farthest wins? No, in America politically speaking, 'the squeaky wheel gets the oil,' so Black America must shout out, "I got next."

Speaking plainly, here in America I don't care to hear one more word about the crisis at the border with immigrants and their problems. I'm not interested in whether the Arab community has to worry about being sent back, deported or any other of their problems. The Dreamers and their problems, I'm not interested. The LGBTQ community and their problems or anybody else's problems, I'm just not interested in hearing about them. Now don't misunderstand me, that doesn't mean I don't care about the problems of others. I'm not saying that. I do care. It's just that I have to keep things in perspective. My people are hurting and have been hurting for a long, long time.

Fortunately, unfortunately, I'm sorry but that's just how I feel and if it offends, so be it. Our blood is running in the streets. The voices of Black America must be heard. I am old enough to recall the look of slavery. My grandparents and older ancestors had a look about them that said just short of defeat. An emptiness that said, you took it all white America.

In America, I have firsthand knowledge of the plight of Black America. Years ago I saw with my own eyes the effects of slavery on my old relatives. They were subservient to whites, flinched at the sight of a white person, the sound of their voice, for no other reason than the color of their skin. Therefore, I have a right to put a chip on my shoulder because I didn't like what I saw, felt.

In the inner city today, Blacks are killing each other at an alarming rate. There is child abuse, sex abuse, drug abuse. It's hard to find a good public school to send kids to. Residents are fearful to walk the streets of the inner city for fear of being robbed, shot, carjacked.

Within this, there is an underlying question for America. At what point does the impact of slavery leave a person? It appears White America made a tall leap. They set the slaves free and figured that's enough. Why should we give them forty acres and a mule? They'll be alright, in the by and by, they'll be just fine. Then again, if not, well, that's okay too.

Let's examine this premise for a moment. Slaves were stolen away from their homeland and forced into slavery in America. They were enslaved not because they were in debt to society, not because they were criminals, not because they were spoils of war, not because they wanted to marry the boss's daughter. They were enslaved to enrich a country founded on freedom and equality, how ironic.

Then after the Civil War, they were suddenly set free and wait, there was no bus ticket back to the motherland waiting, no train ticket to freedomland, no free boat ride, no severance pay, nothing. Slaves were given a pretty speech, 'We hold these truths to be self-evident: that all men are created equally, that they are endowed by the creator with certain unalienable rights; that among these are life, liberty and the pursuit of happiness.' Pretty words, but what did they mean to an ex-slave? Did the words even apply to ex-slaves? Apparently, they did not, not by a long shot.

Were ex-slaves given a PTSD check? The definition of PTSD could easily have originated at the end of slavery. Yet White America saw fit to make that tall leap, just freeing the slaves was enough.

Perhaps thinking, it may not have been better had we never brought them to our shores.

The present state of inner city Black America is not okay and I'm tired. In short, until we get our reparations I will not move, nor give up my seat, my place in line for anybody. Black America's place in line has long been established. We've been waiting since 1865. To some people that's a long time to be panting for anything. White America has suggested, get over it, or more recently, go back. I have news for them, if they wrote the right amount on the check, that's an easy decision for me.

Conveniently pointing out, Blacks were freed in 1865, over 150 years ago. That's a long time to hold a grudge or whatever. Okay but what changed post 1865. First, let's lay out the tall leap made by white America, the hypothesis. *Let us set the slaves free and hope everything works out. Over time even if it doesn't work out, slavery will not be the blame for the plight of Black America. The statute of limitations will absolve America. It will be in the rearview mirror and fading from view. As such, the government does not and will not owe them slaves and their ancestors a penny. In the end, blame whatever the outcome on the Blacks. Brilliant! Just Brilliant!*

It sounded like a reasonable hypothesis. However, let's take a look at the plausibility of this 'great leap.' Did racism disappear? Has discrimination disappeared? Are Blacks treated equally across the board? Are Black people still being lynched? Has the KKK disappeared, other hate groups not been born? Is white nationalism dead in America?

According to researched records, the last known lynching of a Black man occurred on March 21, 1987. Michael Donald was beaten and hung from a tree in Mobile, Alabama. There may have been others. My belief, I'm sure there were others. Rodney King was beaten like a dog on March 3, 1991 in L.A. On June 7, 1997 a Black man, James Byrd, Jr. was dragged to his death by white men in Jasper, Texas.

America, what has changed? On February 5, 2012, 17 year old Travon Martin was shot to death by a white man while walking in his own neighborhood. The only thing in his hands, a pack of Skittles. And the white man that executed him was acquitted, all because he was 'standing his ground.' As if this white man owned the ground where he killed the boy. It wasn't even his yard. All Black parents must pray for their kids to come home safe each night.

In 2018 a white policewoman in Texas shot and killed a Black man in his own apartment. A case of mistaken, 'what's this nigga doing in my house?' Of course, he was unarmed. Did it matter? In 2019 a policeman in Texas killed an unarmed Black woman in her home. A case of 'I thought I saw a boogey man.' In 2020 a Black man jogging was gunned down by white residents in Georgia because he looked, 'suspicious.' Whatever that means. On May 25, 2020, a white policeman in Minneapolis kept his knee on a Black man, George Floyd's neck until he died. He didn't need a rope. The lynching continues. The only thing differently today, with cameras everywhere, the lynchings are harder to conceal.

Of course, this is just a small sampling of what hasn't changed in regards to lynching. The list goes on and on and on. Black people executed for no justifiable reason, other than being Black in America. My ears are waxed closed. I am not going to listen to any more of anybody's problems, not now.

America says reparations is asking for too much. America is quick to look upon highly successful Blacks then suggest, "if they can do it, why can't other Blacks. They're just too lazy." Therefore, even the suggestion of reparations should never be brought up. "It'll never happen, it's impossible. That check will never be written." Well, being told no didn't stop MLK and other civil rights leaders in their quest for civil rights. The denials should not stop Black America's quest for reparations today. If we refuse to listen to the problems of others, then eventually they will listen to ours. Black America must recognize its power.

Some would argue vociferously, today the Blacks are free in America. But can a Black man afford to not look over his shoulder in the wrong part of town? Not keep his hands up when the police arrive on the scene? Further, are Blacks supposed to just accept getting paid a fraction of what white counterparts make? Are they supposed to accept secondhand as new, be alright with the inequities? Just be glad, 'I's free,' even as Black neighborhoods self-destruct and Black people die, suffer.

No, l will not listen to other people's squeaking wheels, no matter their problems. Nor will I join in their parade, not now. I will not set the problems of Black America to the side, accepting, "maybe we can take up reparations next year, next term, when the political climate is more favorable." How can I help these other groups of people, when my wounds are festering? Must we have our heads cracked open, be shot dead, to get this nation's undivided attention? No that's been happening, and America remains silent.

And I'm supposed to hear about everybody else's damn problems, feel their pain and put my pain to the side, to the back. I've seen that movie. My parents and their generation had to sit to the back of the bus. Sit back and accept second class as okay, for being Black in America. Give up their seat to the white woman, even the white man if he so desired.

I'm sorry but that dog won't hunt any more. It's not okay. My feet are tired too. Every time I see a lynching, I feel my ancestors pain resurfacing in my bones. They got home from a long day's work in the fields or in the white man's kitchens, with nothing to show. Settled for scraps, had to take it as if still on a plantation, post 1865. Wasn't okay then and it ain't okay now, not by a long shot.

When are our Black politicians going to stop trying to get along? When are they going to say what needs to be said, to the powers that be, and more importantly to ourselves? It's as if you can't call a spade a motherfucking spade. The question begs an answer. Where are we headed? Many of the boats of Black America are badly listing. Why are our leaders reluctant to grab the mantle for reparations and refuse to let go?

It seems the wrong brothers are dying. The young Black men with their entire future ahead of him, dying in the street. The young Black men sent off to prison, never to return. Their life is over. Innocent Black men and women lynched by corrupt cops, overzealous whites.

If we don't get this right, we're stuck on Groundhog Day. What we don't learn from, we will continue to repeat.

It's appears so easy for our political leaders to go along with the, what's expected, forgo the what is needed. Where is the outrage at the plight of Blacks in America's inner cities? For too long the blame has been put on Black people themselves. Rather we must tie all the ills of Black America to the lingering effects of slavery. And no don't tell me, "Black people have it easy. They are their own worst enemy." Yea but why America? I'm sitting here listening to old school Temptations', "Masterpiece" and I'm wondering, what year is it? Today the plight of Blacks in America is "Masterpiece" 2.0 on steroids.

Don't tell me it's a money thing, reparations will break the bank. America finds money, prints money for what it wants. We send billions annually to aid foreign countries. America has spent untold billions of dollars on foreign wars, the Vietnam War, Iraq War and continued Middle East fighting. Now tell me again, what did we get out of those wars?

Figuratively speaking, Blacks in America have been and continue to be slowly herded onto waiting ships and sent off, not back home to Africa, but to a place I call **Black Man Island**. Where is Black man island? If you're a Black in America. It might be right where you stand.

Something is amiss, the math on the tall leap white America made in 1865 does not work. You steal a people, bring them to a strange land, thousands of miles from their home and illegally enslave them for hundreds of years. Set them free with nothing and that's it. Essentially, they are left to survive and assimilate or maybe let them die off would be okay. Mind you, setting Blacks free in the Jim Crow South could well be considered a death sentence.

Upon gaining their freedom, the prevalent result, at best a sharecropper's life. Left to continue working for next to nothing, the threat of death a clear possibility. Today post 1865, what is the inner city but a modern day plantation for most Blacks?

Post 1865 ex-slaves were left to pass down what to their children, an incomprehensible load from their shoulders to their children's shoulders? So for all the free labor, all ex-slaves had was a chip on their shoulders, well I dare say, it was a log. Take less and accept it as normal, as if more than was deserved.

At the end of slavery, Blacks did not walk off from the plantation shouting, "glory hallelujah, everything is just fine now." They were at best confused. Probably wondering, is this another motherfucking trick? It had to be complicated.

Unfortunately, there were no psychologists to clear the minds of slaves poisoned with this PTSD. Slavery was still fresh on their minds, deep in their souls. There was no monetary benefits package, no severance package or anything else that would have benefited ex-slaves, eased the transition.

Post 1865, how many Black lives must be lost America? To prove that the 'Tall Leap Hypothesis' did not work. Are Blacks doomed as the next 'Red Man' race of people? The population of Native Americans was approximately 60 million in the 1400s. Today their population is less than 6 million. Is that America's goal for Black America?

Today, the list of groups wanting something from this government is long and growing. Who will be first to sacrifice their wants and needs for that of Black America? It should be made abundantly clear. Why should Black America give up their seat, get behind or on the band wagon for any group? Unless and until, all other groups support a deal for reparations for Black America. Anything less for Black America should be a non-starter.

A Home for the Second-Class Citizen

Black Man Island, A place not far from where you are.

It should be noted Black Man Island is not an island in the normal sense. First, let us consider what an island is in the physical sense. An island is a land mass surrounded by water. There is no escape by land from an island. You can't walk off, drive off. If you don't have a boat, you can't sail off. If you don't have a plane, you can't fly off. You're trapped, stuck on the island.

By the same token, an island can also be about isolation, aloneness, separation. Ostracized, ignored, marginalized, you can be alone in a large city, fenced in. You can be made to feel alone in a crowd of people. No one wants any part of you. You have no real friends, allies. It's as if you have the plague. You're made to feel lost and alone. You could just as well be on an island.

Such is the plight of Blacks in America. On the surface Blacks live in America, they are natural born citizens, true Americans. But the reality, Blacks in America are in a constant flux of being isolated, ostracized, made to feel unwanted and un-American, second-class citizens.

Once White America got through with Blacks at the end of slavery, they immediately found ways to keep them in their place, a distinguishable place. Keep them separate and apart in, 'The Bottom,' 'The Hood,' 'The Bricks,' 'Cross the Tracks,' on the 'Westside,' 'Southside,' 'Northside,' on an 'Island,' away from us white folk.

For the purposes of this case: *Black Man Island is the continuous and systematic movement to keep Blacks separate, second-class, apart from mainstream White America, by any means necessary, be it physically, economically, criminally, medically, mentally, educationally, politically; promoted and enforced by White America and even some Black Americans.* And what's worse, to blame the whys on Blacks in America, a case of shameful victim blaming.

The Physical Black Man Island

Where is the physical place called Black Man Island? Go to any city in America, small or large with a sizeable Black population. You'll find a neighborhood of predominantly Black residents. In the smaller cities, you'll find maybe one neighborhood of disadvantaged Blacks. In larger cities, you'll find a multitude of disadvantaged Black neighborhoods. Draw a line around them or mark their boundaries with street names. This area, this section, some call the hood, the ghetto or a directional name, such as the city's northside, eastside, southside, westside. Some might even call it nigga town.

Within these neighborhoods you'll find the larger Black population living at or below the poverty level. Substandard housing is common. Failing schools is the norm. Crime is high. Drug use is rampant. This is 'Black Man Island'. The modern-day replacement for the plantation. It was never intended for slaves to leave the plantation, then mix freely with white folks. Whites and former slave owners did all they could to prevent it.

Today, Blacks in America imagine they're free, but will they ever truly be free? Or are they a doomed people? Trapped on an island from where they can never escape. Simply put, there is a large percentage of White America that does not want Black people anywhere near them. They suggest silently to themselves or publicly aloud, 'keep them across the tracks,' in a section of town not of much value(that is until gentrification begins to set in). Keep them in the projects, in the housing developments. Their thinking, if we can't send them back, though it's not a water barrier, it works. Least we know where they are at all times. The irony of gentrification. It's just a roundabout way of saying, that the land wasn't worth squat when we sold it to you, now we gotta take it back. It's too good for you niggas.

On Black Man Island, police protection is questionable. Maybe the police protection is slow to arrive, if at all. You might wonder should you even call the police? You question, can the police be trusted? Will they come to protect and serve or harm?

The politicians come to Black Man Island infrequently, just for electioneering, maybe to cut a ribbon or two. Then they disappear. As if residents on the island are in a part of the district that is difficult to get to, navigate.

White folks come to Black Man Island only when necessary. You have something they want, that plot of ground, cheap drugs, that vote, all the money in your pocket, that ice cream cone you're holding in your hand. They plot how to get it from you. They may even befriend you. Act as if they know you, like you. They'll do almost anything, they want what you have. When it's gone, you're back in isolation, as if you have the incurable plague.

Some Blacks might think things are changing, 'that was back then, it's 2020, things are different now.' Really? Do white women still cross the street when a Black man approaches? Clutch their purse as he passes? Are Blacks watched closely as soon as they enter certain stores? Do whites still move from neighborhoods as it crowds with Black residents? Question, 'can Blacks afford it, are they selling drugs?' Suggest 'there goes the neighborhood.' Wait, Blacks packing up trying to escape the neighborhood too. Can you blame them? Their feeling, it's just a matter of time before the neighborhood goes caput. They want out. Wait and it won't be worth salvaging.

The Non-Physical Black Man Island

It's a feeling. Blacks in a predominately white city or neighborhood are paid special attention. Maybe you're the only Black in a room with a large number of whites. The stares from the corner of eyes question what are you doing there? If you're the only Black in a group, the conversations are filled with side microaggressions that aren't funny. The color of your skin puts you on an island.

You're standing or sitting in the lunchroom or waiting in a Denny's restaurant surrounded by white people but you're not getting served. No one is talking to you, they're ignoring you, hoping you get the message. You're insignificant to them and then, Blacks maybe buy in. Believing 'maybe, we're not worth being supported.' Blacks become insignificant to themselves, thus adding to the self-destruction of the Black community. Do Blacks even realize this?

Psychological Warfare

Through the years since the civil rights movement, white America has sought to remind Blacks who they are through mental manipulation, no matter where they might live or how much money they have. Fortunate Blacks get off the island with a visa. How do you get a visa? Simple, you need a specialized talent. You can entertain your way off, sing, dance, play sports. If you're smart, you can get a good education, work twice as hard and get off. If you're good looking, you can marry your way off.

Having said all that, physical escape may not be enough. How can you tell if you're still on Black Man Island? Certain whites are not going to just march through town waving a confederate flag. They have taken to the not so subtle jab.

Scenario 1.

Let's say you're driving your new Benz around at two in the morning, just cruising. You're dressed casually. Enjoying the fruits of your labor and you get pulled over by a white cop. He jumps out the cop car and shouts, "Get your ass out of the car." What do you do? You had better show the policeman your hands and get your Black ass out of the car quick. You are on Black Man Island.

Scenario 2.

Let's say you go for a walk. You're in a good mood, so you're smiling as white folk approach. Suddenly they quickly cross the street. You turn around to see if something ominous is behind you. No worries, they are running from your Black ass. You're on Black Man Island.

Scenario 3.

Let's say you've been on a job for a number of years. You do your job and then some. All the while your white counterpart continues to complain, comes to work late, you even have to help pull their weight. By chance they mention their lousy salary. Wait they make more than you. And by the way, you trained them, taught them all they know. Should you walk into your boss's office and bitch? Oh no, you can be replaced. You best believe, it's best you keep quiet, you're on Black Man Island.

Scenario 4.

The police negotiate with potential white culprits but with potential Black culprits its shoot first. Figure out later he was no threat. It may come out later a mistake was made, a fatal mistake. If not for body cameras and cell phone cameras, how many Black lives would truly matter? To stay alive, best you be on guard always. Where the police are concerned you are always on Black Man Island.

Scenario 5.

You're in a room with a bunch of white people. You can't find anyone to talk to. None of the conversations you overhear seems to make sense. No worries, you're on Black Man Island.

Scenairo 6.

You're Black and rich, live up in the hills. But do you dare take off the fancy clothes, take off the expensive jewelry, all the material things that identify you as a rich nigga. Try getting bold, drive to downtown but not in your fancy car, take the bus. Get off the bus and take a stroll down the rich part of Main street where the fancy named stores are located. Do you feel the stares? You walk into a department store, a boutique, a haberdashery. The security guard stares at you. He's letting you know, "I got my eyes on you."

You walk into a luxury auto dealership and you're ignored. The salesmen act as if they don't see you. They're thinking, you're just looking, why waste time?

You walk into the fancy named restaurant and you wait while others around you get served. Pissed you storm out. By the way, that's what they wanted. They didn't like the way you looked, you didn't look like you had the money and you certainly were not going to tip.

Brother, sister, you are on Black Man Island without your notoriety, your entourage, your material things that identify who you are. You could be one of the richest Blacks in America but you're not recognized without all the glitz. You are identified and isolated by your skin color, how you appear. There is no doubt, you are on Black Man Island, and it's a lonely feeling. Hurry home and get back into your comfort zone.

In just the past few years Blacks have been accosted for no apparent reason, other than being Black. Let's check some recent news wires.

Permit Patty: White woman calls police on 8 year old Black girl selling lemonade on the sidewalk.

Barbeque Betty: White woman calls police on Black family barbequing in public park.

Hotel Bob: Hotel Clerk calls police, suspicious Black man is in hotel lobby. The Black man is a hotel guest talking on his cell phone.

Banker Bob: White bank employee calls police on Black man trying to cash his own check.

College Cutie: White employee calls police on Black graduate student eating lunch on campus.

Coed Shirley: White college student calls police on Black girl asleep in her own dorm.

Parker Jane: Park employee calls cops on Black family trying to visit a public park.

Petty Betty: Calls police on birch watcher in Central Park. He was threatening her life cause he told her to leash her dog, follow the rules.

We may have heard about Donald Sterling, previous owner of the Los Angeles Clippers until 2014. His downfall, what he really thought of Black people. He was taped chiding his then girlfriend about her relationships with Blacks. Speaking to her, "it bothers me that you want to broadcast that you're associating with Black people." Of course, his girlfriend was of a mixed race. He went on, "why are you with Black people. Do you have to hang with Magic? Bring him to my games." What? But Magic is a rich nigga. You can't make this shit up.

Colin Kaepernick, former quarterback for the San Francisco 49ers did the unthinkable. Colin essentially said, at the playing of our national anthem, while everyone else is standing, 'I'm gonna take a knee. Until America does something about the police's unfair treatment of Blacks. Why should I stand?' We haven't seen him on a football field since, in a league dominated by Black men. Though he can still play. Well let's put it plainly, the NFL owner of the Houston Texans Bob McNair called players 'inmates.' What is that what you think of the players?

The former first lady Michelle Obama gets called a monkey. The first lady, why attack her? They want her in her place on Black Man Island. They want her to know she will never be white. Guess what, she appears comfortable in her skin. Countless successful Blacks, rich and famous, they appear to have made it in America. But behind the scenes, seems many whites in America had hoped Blacks had never been brought over.

The psychological warfare by White America presses the poor, as well as the rich and successful Blacks to feel uncomfortable, unwelcome through a psychological manipulation. Even if it's not done consciously, it still exists. They just may not see it. Perhaps because it's behavior inherited from their ancestors, commonly referred to as 'white privilege' today.

The poorer Blacks are treated like unwanted pests. Whites don't want them around. Not to drive them around, cut their grass, clean their house, watch their kids. They have found a more acceptable alternative, Latinos and other less intimidating foreigners. The goal is to isolate Blacks by any means possible. And after so many years, Blacks on the Island appear conditioned to act and behave as if they really don't matter. Second class is okay.

There is an invisible fence around every Black in America. The invisible and infamous wall follows Blacks wherever they go. Black Man Island, that visible and invisible place they put you when they don't need you, when they want nothing to do with you. Since the day the Emancipation Proclamation was signed, Black America has been slowly uploaded and unloaded onto Black Man Islands and Blacks don't even realize it. Black people are on an island and most aren't even aware.

Would you be comfortable if you were on a boat with just Blacks, not knowing your destination? Blacks you don't know. No one on board seems to know anything. Everyone on board is wondering, where is this boat headed? You can't get off, you're stuck, surrounded by an unwelcoming ocean.

You sit, feeling trapped. Anxiety, fear set it, is an escape possible, who would help with an escape? Looking around as the boat drifts away from shore, "is anyone with us? Does anyone really care?" Those on the mainland know your plight, they can see you're in trouble. You try to get their attention, stare at them, wave at them, as you sail away. You are ignored, they choose to look the other way.

Blacks are sailed away to an Island not of their choosing, without their direct knowledge or permission, and no one will throw out a lifeline. Unloaded to a place for no other reason than their skin color. The objective of Black Man Island becomes obvious, to isolate Blacks. To make Blacks feel uncomfortable, as if they are so different that they do not belong in white society. Make Blacks feel second class. Make Blacks feel as if they need to go back to where they belong, if not back to Africa, to a Black Man Island. "You'll feel better where you belong." White America always suggesting, they know what's best for Blacks.

In short, Black America has been had, hoodwinked and bamboozled. If Black Man Islands are so good, then why are the conditions what they are? Nevertheless, if the problems of Black America are not addressed, the cancer that is indigenous to Black Man Islands will continue its spread to all America.

The Posthumous Testimony

400 Years of Struggles

<u>Stolen Away</u>

You might imagine one day Africans were walking along in their native land. It was a day like any other. Maybe they were asleep. Perhaps working fields to feed their families, fishing along the coast, hunting the jungles. Then suddenly, without warning they were trapped, captured by slave traders. Maybe they were captured by their African enemies, then sold to slave traders.

Once captured most of these Africans ended up in the holding cells of prisons along Africa's Gold Coast. Later they would be hoarded onto waiting slave ships. Stripped of clothes and shaved, the men were chained like criminals, animals. Theses cramped wooden slave ships housed 250-600 Africans. Before long they set sail for a grueling journey lasting 2-3 months. Stolen away from their homeland and stored as new-found treasure, spoil.

Over the course of the slave trade, lasting approximately 3 1/2 to 4 centuries, some estimates are that 10-12 million slaves were brought to North America. It was a grueling trip. Many lives were lost. During this period, over 1-2 million captured slaves died in transit. Disease was prevalent. Many slaves tried to end their journey through suicide-starvation or by simply jumping overboard. If successful, you might consider them the lucky ones.

The Middle Passage

The crossing of the Atlantic as you might imagine on slave ships was brutal. Slaves spent most of their time crammed into crowded ship hulls. Forced to defecate right where they were. The men were beaten to discourage mutiny. The women at the disposal of the crew were raped repeatedly.

These barbaric conditions were mostly concealed or ignored. Did the world care, four hundred years is a long time? Undoubtedly not, the ill-gotten gains of slave labor clouded the world's views and opinions. Living in nothing less than pig sties, effectively these slaves were nothing more than animals.

Slavery: A fate worse than death.

Once the slaves landed, they were cleaned up and prepared for transition. These captives may have thought the worst was over. They arrived on dry land and their treatment was mostly worse. They were put in pens until new owners came and took them away. Or they were quickly sent to auctions to be sold off. If they arrived with other family members, separation was given no thought. Prospective new owners pried and pricked them like horses to judge their strengths. A strong buck was prized for work and mating. A woman of child-bearing age a valuable commodity for reproduction.

The Transition

Upon arriving on the plantation, over the course of the next 2-3 years, the new slaves had to undergo a transition. Language barriers had to be overcome. Their new tasks on the plantation had to be spelled out. For this process, they were mostly turned over to the Slave Overseer. He had a method to his madness. Beatings and torture were his tools.

It seems his goal was dehumanization. Get them to believe they were nothing more than circus animals. Train them to be subservient, that's how you get the most out of these trained animals. Once trained, these humanoid machines were available to be worked at beck and call.

During this transition, the men were beaten, treated like dogs in training, less than a man. The women were beaten and raped without regard. The overseer knew when he had succeeded. A less than human slave appeared destroyed, brainwashed.

Slaves were conditioned to live with the least, in cramped huts, in mostly shabby housing. Some slaves were forced to make their own living accommodations with minimal materials supplied them. Slaves were given minimal clothing, maybe a pair of shoes a year and a few pair of underwear a year. To survive most slaves were given scraps off the table, the refuse.

Slaves were forced to work from sunrise to sunset. Inside the plantation house, women did all the cleaning, cooking, ironing. Still both men and women worked the fields. Some plantations might give their slaves a day off each Sunday, some a day off a month, while others didn't get a day off.

To keep slaves in check, ignorant, most southern states passed antiliteracy laws. It was against the law to teach slaves to read and write. This stifling of their education was just another way to keep control of the slaves. The slave owner's thinking, "I'll tell you what you need to know." These laws were punishable with jail time.

Family life was suspect, there might be a father owned by one slave owner and the mother and child owned by another. Mothers worked until they gave birth and returned to work soon after giving birth. There was little time for nurturing. Slavery made family bonding difficult, if not impossible. And by the way, it was not uncommon for children to be ripped from their mother's arms. They were owned animals, so reproduction was about money, creating wealth.

The Economics of the Southern Plantation

Prior to slavery the south was probably an afterthought to Northerners. The south lacked the social graces and sophistication of the country's north, which was mostly Northeastern and Missouri Valley states. Prior to slavery the south was comprised of mostly dirt poor farmers, not fit to carry the northerner's bags.

Slavery changed that. Slaves were tools, machines, pushed to the brink. A slave dies, replace him. If a plantation had any number of slaves, how could a plantation, a farm with no slaves compete against it? It was impossible. Pressed to work like machines, slaves produced untold wealth for southerners and the south. The mistreatment of a slave was a small and insignificant price to pay and so southern states flourished. The south's thirst for wealth could not be satisfied.

A House Divided

As if being a slave was not enough, slave owners worked to create animosity amongst the slaves. The slave master had his favorites and these slaves were rewarded. If you kissed master's ass enough, ratted out other slaves, you got a plumb job on the plantation. Maybe drove the missus around in her buggy, worked in the cool of the plantation house or oversaw the field niggas.

Slaves that worked inside the plantation house were considered 'house niggas' while slaves that worked the field were considered 'field niggas'. This purposeful division caused resentment, whereas the house niggas looked down upon the field niggas. And the field niggas resented the house niggas who thought they were special, they had it too easy. The niggas that ratted on other slaves were thought to be Uncle Toms, a sellout. They were generally hated by all slaves.

It was not uncommon for slave women to be raped on a regular basis by their overseer, the slave master or slave owner. The slave woman had no recourse but to allow this to happen. Rejection meant beating or death. Afterall, slave women were owned property.

The offspring of the white slave owner was easily distinguishable because of the lightness of their skin. These unwanted pregnancies created tensions amongst the slaves, as if the slave woman had freely allowed this to happen. She might even be despised.

The light skinned slave was looked down upon by the darker slaves. Even hated because they may have been favored by the owner or overseer. The light-skinned slaves disliked the darker skinned slaves, avoided them at all cost, because dark was bad. This ugly remnant of slavery, light versus dark skinned Blacks existed within Black America for decades and is still prevalent to an extent even today.

The 'Willie Lynch' breeding method was to sow hate and envy amongst plantation slaves, force them to rely upon the white man, 'he's your friend.' Separated by how you looked, the work you did. These divisions pitted slaves against each other, thus giving birth to the 'crab mentality' that holds Blacks down. This colorism is a huge problem even today.

The Emancipation Proclamation

At the signing of the Emancipation Proclamation, there were approximately 3.1 million slaves freed. The north had won the war between the states and slaves were freed by then President Lincoln. But was it really about all men being created equal or was it about economics? Did Lincoln truly care about the plight of slaves or were slaves the byproduct of holding the Union together?

The economy of the south was built on slavery and was flourishing. The mansions lined the boulevards and the grand plantations lined the bayous and countryside. Who wouldn't be envious of the flourishing southern lifestyle? Every slave purchased or bred had to produce, from the little ones that fanned the resting missus, to the old mammie that ran the house. All had a purpose. Slave owners and their children had it easy, they didn't have to lift a finger.

The white northerners began to feed a changing narrative, 'these Black men are our equal, they are not property.' Or was it more about undercutting these undereducated, uncouth southerners down to size. At any rate, the slaves were freed, free but what then.

Forty Acres and a Mule

What were freed slaves promised? Upon the signing of the Emancipation Proclamation, reparations were discussed. History tells us General William Tecumseh Sherman set aside 400,000 acres to be divided up into parcels no larger than 40 acres for freed slaves.

Further the federal government would provide mules to farm the land, hence the 'Forty acres and a mule.'

Land was to be given to the freed slaves, to live on, to farm. Had it been followed through on, can you imagine the effect this would have had on Blacks in America? Can you imagine the wealth that would have been created by these freed Blacks. Ex-slaves would have ownership and been put in control of land to farm, build cities. They would be performing work they had become adept at, thusly creating untold wealth for themselves and their heirs.

But it never happened. President Andrew Johnson successor to President Lincoln squashed any notion. The new president saw no reason to take the land of white men and give it to slaves. Regardless of whether they deserved the land or not. Possibly he was thinking, why take land from our white southern brothers to give to lowly slaves?

The irony of reparations is that slaveowners wanted them and some received compensation. In Washington D. C. the government agreed to pay $300 per freed slave to slaveowners. Imagine that, slave owners that profited from slavery were compensated for losing their free labor. Do you suppose that's when the phrase 'only in America' came about?

The Initial Shock

As one might imagine, the sudden end to slavery was probably unexpected and shocking to the freed slaves. They wondered, "are we really free? Don't play with me?" One day you're beaten and worked like a slave and the next day you're free. Kicked off the plantation with just the rags on their back, now what? Reality kicked in. Perplexed they wondered, where do we go from here? There was no bus ticket waiting, no severance pay, no resettlement plan.

Unfortunately, many ex-slaves simply starved or died of disease. Left to scavenge for food, live in unsanitary camps. The Union soldiers that remained in the south seemed to care little for their plight. One wonders, was the war really fought over slavery as inhumane? The inhumane treatment of Blacks did not end. A singular alternative emerged for ex-slaves, go back to the planta-tions and work for essentially nothing. Get charged room and board for paltry food and squalid living conditions.

Soon after the war, reconstruction was established by the north. Carpetbaggers swooped in and took the best. Set up pseudo Black officials, a temporary kangaroo government. There was resent-ment of Blacks by southern whites. The wealth of southerners dissipated. Their opulent livelihood was gone. Their land was snatched away, all because of slavery. In a shocking twist to slav-ery, southerners blamed the victims, the slaves for their predicament. There would be hell to pay.

The Jim Crow Era

As reconstruction ended, southern whites resorted to retaliatory practices and created discriminatory laws. Laws that mandated separation of races in all public places, schools, restaurants, bath-rooms, parks. Southerners were thinking, if we have to live with them, let's keep them separate, on an island. Hence, segregation was the law of the land. 'Colored only', 'white only' signs on doors became the norm.

These laws became known as the Jim Crow laws. The name Jim Crow a take-off of the old term, 'Jump Jim Crow'. Whereby a white man in Black face satirized the slave acting a fool. Treatment of Blacks remained close to that of slavery times. Blacks were free but they had to cross the street when whites approached. Hold their heads low, don't look a white man in his eyes. Blacks were not supposed to live above whites. That would be sacrilegious, a possible death sentence.

Blacks were given the right to vote in 1870 but southern Blacks were mocked when they showed up to polls to vote. They were asked to pay a poll tax or given a literacy test they couldn't pass. Essentially, they were turned away. This despite the fact many whites could not read or write in the south. The white southern-ers supposed, what nerve of them to ask.

Bottom line, Jim Crow laws were created to keep Blacks separate and they would never be considered equal. Fact is, if most southern whites had their way, they would have obliterated all Blacks from the south. It should also be known, Blacks remained in the south not because they liked it, but because of economics. They could scarcely afford to leave.

The Migration

The mistreatment of Blacks and lack of opportunity in the south set forth a migration of Blacks. They wanted out of this plantation system of the south. Ex-slaves wanted a better life for themselves and their children, a better home, a better education. So around 1916 southern Blacks began migrating to the north, midwest and west. This migration lasted into the late 1960s. Certainly, the better jobs were there but not everyone was happy to see Blacks arrive. Roadblocks were thrown all along the way. Blacks dug in, they had arrived and weren't going back. The Jim Crow north was not as bad as the Jim Crow south.

The Civil Rights Era

Gradually, liberal leaning whites and Blacks began to work for equal rights for all Blacks. Blacks tired of being kicked around began to make demands of the country. Something had to give. In 1955 Rosa Parks sat on a bus in Montgomery, Alabama and decided she had had enough. She wasn't giving up her seat as ordered by a white man. Her defiance put a face on the civil rights movement. Defiantly Blacks took to the streets to boycott. The bus boycotts lasted over a year.

Civil rights victories were difficult. Despite the 1954 landmark supreme court decision Brown versus The Board of Education of Topeka, segregation remained embedded in the south. Southern governors such as George Wallace of Alabama refused to allow integration. His clarion call was, "segregation now, segregation tomorrow, segregation forever." Thankfully, the federal government soon put a stop to his stance. White folks didn't get it, they figured Blacks had some fine 'colored' institutions, why do they need to apply to 'our lily-white' institutions?

These were difficult times in America, many Blacks and some white sympathizers were beaten, some murdered for civil rights. To many, slavery had never ended. Fortunately, with the steady hands of civil rights leaders, Blacks refused to let anyone turn them around. Leading to the passage of historic civil rights legislation in 1964.

Post Civil Rights Era

The 1970s brought an unwelcome change for white America. Blacks were making economic inroads. They could enroll at any school and live anywhere. Still there was intimidation. Moving into certain neighborhoods for Blacks meant a burning cross planted on their front lawn or maybe a visit from the KKK, maybe some other white neighborhood organization.

White America worked hard to keep Blacks physically in certain areas, isolated. It was never the aim of white America to put the better, let alone the equal in the' colored' sections. Simply put, the plantation had evolved into the 'hood', 'the ghetto', a picture of hopelessness, blight, second class. Still whites couldn't figure out why Blacks appeared dissatisfied.

The white establishment worked to develop new ways to force isolation, skirt around legislation. As Blacks ventured out from these new plantations, mental intimidation was the norm. When burning a cross became illegal, the white man created other means. Outright discrimination in plain sight, redlining, housing discrimination, loan discrimination, job discrimination, it was anything goes. Run a thread through the years, the underlying efforts of white America has been separation by any means necessary. Then again, what was the purpose of segregation? To keep Blacks away, not to keep level the playing field.

When all else failed, whites moved further and further away from the cities. Then appeared mystified that Blacks showed up wanting the same thing. Today whites knowingly can't burn a cross in your yard but they put their confederate flag out in front their house. They can put the Trump sign out in front or some other Republican, white nationalist symbol. They will call the cops on Blacks for no reason at all. They know they can't get rid of Blacks but they send clear messages. Stay where you belong, on the plantation, Black Man Island. Or get ready to be uncomfortable. History is not repeating itself. It never changed. The fundamental problems created by the slavery system have not changed, is not changing.

400 years after the first slaves arrived, what has changed from the plantations of yesteryear and the Black Man Islands of today? Black children of the inner city are born into poverty and are being scarcely educated. Housing is mostly substandard. Healthcare is questionable. Opportunity for good paying jobs is sparse. Young men are being ripped from their mother's arms by injustice. Seldom is a father figure in the home. Black lives did not matter then, do they matter today? And the government still appears oblivious to change a damn thing.

Color of a Name

The Reflection America Doesn't' Want to Look at

Why has it been so difficult for Blacks to assimilate into the culture of America, feel one with America? I mean respected, fully accepted, as American as apple pie. What is it about this Black skin, brown skin, almost white skin? Is it a color thing or a lingering slavery thing?

It can't be just about color. Africans that migrate to the U.S. don't arrive to the U.S. with that slavery chip or log on their shoulder. They appear to see things differently. They believe this is a great country, not without fault but a country of opportunity. They may very well question, why are Blacks unwilling to take full advantage? Likewise, immigrants of color come to the U.S., don't complain or look for excuses as to why things are so bad for non-whites.

These non-white immigrants go for it, work hard and do well, send money back home to support their families back home. They don't seem to understand Black Americans. They are quick to point out, "if you saw how we live in our country, you would be so happy to be here in America." Ergo, it's not a color thing.

It would appear most foreigners don't get the slavery thing. Their apparent thinking, it happened so long ago, it's an excuse at best. Of course, they know there is discrimination. There will always be discrimination. There is discrimination everywhere, between the rich and poor, one tribe versus another, one religion versus another, one neighborhood versus another, north versus south, east versus west. In America, land of the free, home of the brave, you just move on, deal with it. They don't see these lead shoes Blacks perceive are on their feet from birth.

Whites here in America see things differently also. Their attitude, what's wrong with Blacks? They want everything handed to them on a silver platter, free this, free that. For the most part, they're thinking, if Blacks would only get off their ass and go to work, stay in their place, it would be a better country. Whatever that means, well we can surmise it means stay on your Black Man Islands.

Why is slavery still the elephant in the room? No one wants to address its lasting effects and it's white-washed when taught in schools. No one wants to acknowledge its cost to Black America. Even if Blacks as a people are not over it, doesn't seem to matter. Why can't Blacks continue the discussion? After all Blacks were the victimized. Why blame the victims? Why should it be over just because white America and the rest of the world says, "it happened so long ago, Blacks need to move on. This is the land of opportunity. Make your own breaks. Why cry over spilled milk?"

At the same time, no one is questioning the #metoo movement. If a woman was assaulted when she was a young girl, a teenager, a young woman and she's now an old lady, so be it. Let her speak. Justice must be served. Decades old abuse cases are being dealt with.

What about the perverted catholic priests? The catholic church long sought to keep buried their dirty little secret. Eventually victims came to light. Memories of young boys abused came to the surface. Decades old abuse cases came to light. The perverts were sought out and sent to jail if they were not already jailed or dead. The catholic church has spent over a billion dollars to settle sex abuse cases thus far. Was there any hesitation to right the wrongs after they came to light? No, it should be done, it had to be done.

What about that National Treasure, that sacred institution, the Boy Scouts of America? They recently came under scrutiny and attack for alleged sex abuse against young boys by scout leaders. At minimum, the cases are into the thousands. The abuse dating back decades have estimates of nearly 8,000 boy scout leaders being accused of sex abuse. Estimates are that over 12,000 boy scouts have been abused, dating back 72 years. And now the BSA have filed for bankruptcy protection from pending lawsuits.

What about Jews and the memory of World War II death camps? Jewish survivors never stopped searching for German war crime officers that might have escaped prosecution. The faces of these officers could not be forgotten. Despite the years passing, the changing of names, plastic surgery, memories of their faces could not be erased. Affected Jews skin crawled at the sight of these men, as if they wanted their eyes scratched out. You couldn't blame them.

For good reason, there is no statute of limitations for murder. With the latest technology of DNA and forensics, decades old murders are being solved. Through ancestry DNA, murderers that were roaming free for decades are being brought to justice, some sick and in wheelchairs. No one is feeling sorry for these culprits. If only there was a way to recoup the years of freedom they stole, the only regret.

Today in 2020, still when Blacks think of what their slave ancestors went through it stands to reason, their blood boils. An inherited reaction, they did not experience slavery firsthand. Blacks don't like talking about slavery, watching it on tv. It's a painful truth, though they feel no whips across their backs. There is blood that forever connects slaves and their ancestors that spans forever.

If a Black hears the 'N' word thrown out their way by a racist white, they are ready to go off. The hate spewed behind that word brings out memories of what was done to their mothers and fathers, grandparents, great, great, grandparents. What they had to endure. How hard they had to strive just to survive. The hate coming from the racist dogs that inherited its core meaning makes the skin of Blacks crawl today. That rage that boils inside Blacks at just the hearing of the 'N' word from a racist is also inherited. How else can it be explained?

Blacks can call a white man names, 'cracker', 'white trash', 'honky.' But that does nothing to simmer the boil that originates from thoughts of what was done to their ancestors, the physical and mental abuse. Back in the day and as late as the 1990s, maybe later, if a Black man heard the 'N' word he might break out in a mad dash for fear of his life. Today he might still flinch at hearing the 'N' word in the wrong neighborhood. Compound that by the outright theft of property, physical and intellectual and you might understand the Black man's angst. The plight and the injustice done leaves an indelible impression not easily forgotten.

There is no statute of limitations for murder. How many Black men and women were murdered at the hands of white slave owners and racist whites? Whipped to death, lynched from trees in town, in the woods, in front family and friends. Estimates put the total at nearly 3,500. Lynched for no reason, any reason. Lynched for not working hard enough, for not jumping high enough, talking back, looking back. Oh yeah, lynched for whistling, looking at a white woman. Lynched because they were lied upon. What has been the compensation for the countless murder victims?

How many Blacks have been gunned down for no reason, when a rope wasn't accessible? How many Blacks were wrongly imprisoned through the years, some put to death because of a failed judicial system. Can we get justice for the Blacks wrongly convicted, unjustly murdered? If not now, when?

How much is owed for the free slave labor? Slaves were known to work seven days a week, from sunrise, to sunset, in some cases working 365 days a year. Not given a decent meal, a decent home, let alone a simple thank you.

How do we total up damages for discrimination? Blatant for so many years and still occurring today. How many Blacks were told you're not qualified for the job, the loan, to get into this school? Though they were overqualified.

How do we total the harm done to families, separated by slave owners? How do we total harm done to slave women, brutally raped? They were legally owned property, but did that justify the abuse? If they dared to object, they were beaten or worse murdered. Mattered little to the racist slave owner. His feeling, the only good nigga is a dead nigga. Given virtually no time off for childbirth, child bonding. Black women weren't given time to deal with postpartum depression. Women were expected back in the fields immediately after childbirth. Let's be clear, a good dog was treated better than a slave.

How do we total up these damages owed Black America? Why can't Black Americans sue this government, that has failed Black America in so many ways? Would a trillion dollars, five trillion dollars be sufficient to make Black America whole, satisfy the debt? Why can't we discuss the matter before congress, the supreme court? Why is it when money for reparations gets brought up the goal posts seem to move?

If only America had just addressed slavery reparations in 1865, just given the negro a few acres, a few dollars, a mule. How could anyone today question America's treatment of ex-slaves, the condition of Black America? The deal would have been cut with the aggrieved parties. If it wasn't a good deal, too bad.

How much wealth did slaves create in this country? Was it asking too much to just be given a small fraction of that wealth? What would the south look like had it not been for slaves? Recently some Blacks and political activists felt it important to remove a few statues of confederate leaders and that was like asking too much. Sadly, this is too little, too late. Only reparations can satisfy the insurmountable injustice of slavery and ensuing mistreatment of Blacks in America.

What's in a name?

Why are these Black people seemingly discounted by the world? Slighted, minimized, have they no value? Cheated on the regular, offered less as acceptable for so long, for no apparent reason except the color of their skin. Expected to accept less and scourged if they complained.

Who are these people? The names have changed but not much more. There seems to have always been a search for identity, verification by a name. When they arrived, that African name just wasn't going to work in America. They were given names by their slave owner. Given a name at the whim of the slave owner.

To the white man they were Black Africans, darkies. Called Negros, a derivative of the Spanish word for Black, negro. Called Niger, a Latin word for Black. Uppity southern whites fashioned Negra, Negress if you were female.

But when did the 'N' word become derogatory? When did it become offensive? Who said it was offensive? Perhaps it occurred when the user began to spit demeaning hatred behind it. Then again, simply put, it's offensive because it's not a person's given name, yet their name seemed irrelevant.

Then the negro was deemed 'colored,' a harmless description of non-whites. Blacks were shades of color, not white. Just don't call them whitish. Colored was thought to be more respectable. It was said President Lyndon Johnson was the last president to use the term Negro to identify Blacks. Before he left office, he's said to have used the term Blacks, a small concession from a southern white.

Blacks in America seemed determined and decided, they would name themselves. We were soul brothers and soul sisters. During the civil rights movement, some Blacks figured an empowering name was needed, the Black Man emerged, giving rise to 'Black Power.' Then they were African Americans, a name popularized by Black leaders in the 1980s. Who are they now? What's next, Native Blacks? Or just call us Black. Drop the American. Just don't call us by the 'N' word, nigga. But then again who are we?

How did you come up? Now if you my boy, it's okay, you my nigga. Old uncle just out of slavery referred to a nigga not by the color of his skin but how he carried himself. "That's a nigga for you. Just look at that nigga." What would they have to say about a young Black man walking, running down the street holding his pants just below his asshole? Easy, "that's a nigga for you."

It appears Blacks have been constantly searching for an identify that can elevate them. During slavery times, they couldn't name themselves nor their offspring. That was master's right. Call him Rover, call her Tootsie and they had better roll on command.

What name is befitting this race that wants to name itself? Wanting to be more, wanting to go higher, to a higher status, wanting a more appealing label, a justifiable legacy. Wanting to distance themselves from any connection to slavery, from the origins of the 'N' word?

So what's the difference between a Black man and a nigga? The clothes he wears, how he acts, carries himself, where he lives? Or does it depend on who uses the word, their purpose? Does the person change one way or the other depending on which he is called? Is he one in the same person, a Black man and a nigga? Does it even matter?

Would Blacks fare better if a they learned a foreign language and identified as Hispanic, Asian, Japanese? Put 'other' than Black on their child's birth certificate. Put other on the job application, rental application, even if you look Black, would that pay? It's easy to understand why some mixed Blacks are quick to distance themselves from being Black, the Black bloc that identifies as Black American. America places no apparent value on being Black in and of itself in America.

But truth crushed to the earth will rise again. We keep trying to bury slavery and it keeps bubbling to the surface. The eroding condition of Black America is a cancer and its spreading. Slavery keeps bubbling back to the surface and is evident in Black America's worsening conditions. The overt actions and behavior of some Black Americans belie the blatant fact that Black America has not gotten over slavery, can't brush past slavery, not by a long shot. The malaise of slavery is in the soul of Black America and it will never die until confronted and dealt with by all America.

What is the value of a name? Is there any consolation in being called Black American, Black, Colored, Soul Brother, when you're called something else behind your back, in private? Wearing Black face yesterday and speaking vehemently against it today? Using racial epithets when you think the camera is turned off, then apologizing in front the camera but under your breath saying something else. Are we devalued by a name? Are Blacks labeled as less by a name, a system that was slavery yesterday, today, forever? There is no color inside the 'N' word. There is just this history to the name.

Growing up in the south, young Black boys were terrorized by older white boys. The whites thought it was funny. So Blacks supposed to just forget about that. Black mothers slaved in the white man's kitchen day and night. Came home worn out with little to show, then had to work in her own house. We're supposed to forget about that. Grown Black men called boy by white boys. We're supposed to forget about that. We're supposed to just forget about the Scottsboro Boys, Will Brown, Emmett Till, Fred Hampton, the Birmingham Church bombing, the Philadelphia bombing. We can't. We shouldn't. That's our history. Is there another history we can pass down to our children? Just conveniently omit the bad parts of our history. Black lives apparently don't matter, not today, not yesterday.

How do we change the narrative, cause we can't change the history? We don't want to change our history. We want reparations to make amends for the wrongs of history. Give us reparations America, the help needed to overcome the wrongs.

What if every Black man and woman had a great job, a pocket full of money, money in the bank, owned vast amounts of real estate? What would happen if every Black family were donned in fine threads? Drove off in a fine automobile. They might get called the 'N' word but the word would not have teeth.

The semantics of the 'N' word would change. It wouldn't be, 'that's a nigga for you' but rather, 'can you believe that nigga?' 'What does he have that I don't have?' The look on the face of the sender of hate would be that of jealousy and envy. Call him what you will but the 'N' word bounces off his back. The Black man might even reply, "do you know who I am?" There is a pride that cannot be denied inside folks that can take good care of themselves and their family. Live the all too elusive American Dream. Is that asking too much America?

A name is who you are, who you represent, not so much on the outside but the inside. Who do you represent? Whose child you are? I believe there was one thing that made the racists hate Dr. King more than anything. We can only estimate how many times he was called the 'N' word, a thousand, ten thousand. It did not appear to change him one bit. It certainly did not deter him though that was the intent.

Dr. King appeared to look upon the senders of the 'N' word with pity, not hate. He saw ignorant fools. They railed against him, he smiled. They had no idea, didn't know who he represented. They stayed focused on the outside. He focused on the inside, was fully confident in who he was, who he represented. He was a child of God. He served a God that did not judge him by the color of his skin but the content of his character. Character, not the name, how we see ourselves, that's what matters.

PART III. THE REPERCUSSIONS OF INJUSTICE

THE ERODING BLACK FAMILY

Seems it was only yesterday, only yesterday. Blacks were proudly marching in the streets for their civil rights. MLK was on the front line, talking bout, 'I have a dream,' that he may not get to see but surely it was coming. Malcolm was spitting out power 'by any means necessary.' The Reverend Jesse Jackson took hold of the mantle and invoked into Blacks a new dictum, "I am somebody."

In 2020, we have Black billionaires in America. A Black man just left the white house as the president of these United States. Would MLK be amazed, dumbstruck or was this the dream he so eloquently spoke of? Surely the 'chickens have come home to roost' in America, as Malcolm so boldly foretold.

However, this is juxtaposed to another grim reality of Black America. As you cast a broad look upon the landscape of Black America, one must ask, are the vast majority of Blacks just crabs in a bucket? A few get out and give the rest their ass to kiss. The crab's parting words, "you are on your own." Meanwhile those still struggling to get out of the bucket latch on for dear life to anyone attempting an escape. The result, a continuous falling back into the crab bucket.

What happened to Black America? Seems as if someone pulled the rug out from under Black America. Upon which a grim discovery was found, seems underneath Black America is an ever-crumbling foundation not suitable to build upon a damn thing, not even a dream.

The plight of Black America is well documented. With all the doors opened, the successes spurred by our ancestors, it would appear on the surface, we are our own worse enemy. We have digressed, fallen further behind. Take your pick or where do you want to start?

During slavery, a Black child might not know their parents, maybe its mother for a short while. The slave owner might sell a father on a whim. Maybe an owner would borrow a strong buck from a neighboring farm to impregnate his mares? Then dispense the Buck back to his neighbor. Then again, a slave owner could rip a young child from his mother's arms and sell the child. The slave owner saw no value in keeping a slave's family intact. So throughout slavery, a slave's family, why what's that?

After slavery that changed. There was courting, Black marriage was expected. Up until the 1950s an overwhelmingly majority of Black families were headed by a married couple. It was a team, a father and mother working together to raise a family. Tradition was for the father and mother to marry and stay married, till death, least try hard. Black folks took their vows seriously, for better or worse. Though the Black family typically didn't have much to begin with and life was mostly worse.

What happened? Since those days there has been a steady decline in the percentage of Black married couples and a corresponding steady rise in Black families headed by a single female. **According to the latest U.S. government statistics, the percent of Black households headed by single mothers was over 70%. In the Black community, 72% of births are out of wedlock.**

What affect has the absence of a father had on Black children, the families, to the Black community? Today we watch as young Black men without a father in the home are more likely to be lost to or gunned down in the unforgiving streets. They are more likely to not finish high school. If they finish high school, many are unable to find gainful employment. Young boys without a father are more likely to find the bottle or some other drug than a job. Discouraged because the inner city streets are empty of opportunity and encouragement, they are more likely to engage in crime. The money in the street is just too tempting and the options too few.

Back in the day, there was discipline in the home. Kids weren't allowed to go anywhere unless they looked presentable. You had to comb your hair. Tuck that shirt in. Today, young men walk around with their pants hung low, hair uncombed and that's a fashion statement. Young girls walk around with everything on display, leaving nothing to the imagination. Sex is like a hiccup. Teenage girls compete to get pregnant. Black women can't seem to find an eligible man. There is a shortage. Can this trend be reversed? Or is that the purpose of a Black Man Island, to eliminate hope of a Black family?

Black Man

There is a reason why derogatory terms exist in the dictionary. I speak of myself. I fell short. I know how that looks. So if the shoe fits, are we supposed to say, it hurts because we don't like the way the shoes looks on our feet? I get tired of watching Black women dragged down by a sorry no good Black man. Be truthful, you know more than one woman in a bad situation. You know how the story goes, 'I can do bad all by myself.' Yet it does not seem to change the plight of so many Black women. They will not leave their 'man,' a subjective term.

What do you call a Black man that will control his woman, what she wears, where she goes, who she talks to, what she does with the money she makes? Will deny her opportunity to better herself, will hold her back. All done so that he might appear large and she small. And this man is supposed to be the leader of the family. Which is why so many Black families are led by the mama, I suppose.

What does Black love mean? To take abuse from a man because he has a convenient penis. What happened to working together to build and not tear down. Are we supposed to give a Black man a pass because he gives good sex, looks good in a t-shirt? Or because he used to be good in sports, was popular in school, was a good catch? But good sex and 'used to be' don't cut it when baby needs new shoes or needs to be fed.

Are we as Black men supposed to give a Black man a pass because it's a Black man thing, you just wouldn't understand? Is there another name we can use to describe this type of Black man? Let's check out Webster's dictionary see if we can find him. A cad, a heel, a rascal, a rogue, they all seem too mild. Or we can settle, he's just a sorry ass nigga.

Why can't we replay the scene of Celie in the Color Purple? All Black women know it by heart, "until you do right by me, everything you think about is going to crumble. Everything you think about is going to fail." Create a public announcement with that scene. Air it on BET network, all the urban radio stations. Put Black men on notice, keep Black men on edge. Played in the background is some Aretha Franklin, 'Do right woman, do right man,' or some 'Respect.'

Saying all that, we would be remiss if we did not explore the why behind the demise of so many of our Black men. Why is abandonment of the family so prevalent in the Black community? We search for an explanation that satisfies.

What are we to expect of our Black men who come from the slave system in America that still exists in some regards? Are we to not believe that the residuals of Willie Lynch's how to make and keep a slave do not exist today? In slavery times, where family was concerned, a Black man was used to propagate the hen house. That's it, there was no requirement to tend the family he created. A Black man could be sold from his family with no regard. If Blacks were told anything by master it was, "what's love got to do with it?" He was given no means to support his family, if he had a family. A slave didn't own a damn thing, so how could he be expected to take care of a family? In short, a Black man was given little regard above the family dog.

It would be a grave mistake to assume that most Black men are just no good by design. That Black men want to be rogues, rascals, low down. Rather we in America must recognize the remnants of slavery are in the Black man's DNA. There is an inherited tendency for Black men to stand behind the Black woman in difficult times and not in front. To rely upon her for whatever. That's who the slavery system in America made Black men to be. And every Black man does not have the strength to break free this design. They are not that strong.

The Black Woman

So let's flip this. So a Black woman is supposed to watch her man get beaten down like a no good dirty dog. Get belittled, talked down to as if he's just below a dog. Watch her man crumble as her master drags her away, to rape her, abuse her. Watch as her man has to play dumb to avoid a beat down. Watch her man get sold off, snatched away, never to be seen again, with not even a good-bye. Watch her Black baby boys get snatched away not even fully weened.

Watch her man get strung up in front her face, in front his kids. And she's not supposed to feel a thing, not feel hurt, pain, nothingness, not cry, plead for him, not feel anguish, not feel attachment, not feel for her man, not want to hold her man, love her man, cry for her man, want to do something for her man but she is helpless and unable to. The Black slave woman stood by helpless, as her children watched in fear and confusion.

It's so easy to sit back and exclaim, "look at that dumb bitch. Letting that nigger walk all over her." This is not normal today or is it? That was then, this is now. Yet it looks all too familiar to a slave system still in existence in America. Black women were made to be the rock of the Black family.

Today a Black man gets beaten, shot down by the cops, by his own brothers. Beaten down by a society that looks down upon him as less than a man, unintelligent and lazy. The Black man has to go out and work twice as hard and end up with half as much. Can't get a job, no one is hiring his kind. Can't get off drugs, can't beat it. Does anyone care, give a damn? His Black woman cares, and we wonder why?

Black boys get snatched away from their mothers by the streets, like those snatched away long ago by slave masters. Does it really matter now, did it mater then? Did America do anything back then, is it doing anything now? A Black mother's love is unconditional, expecting nothing in return, not even love. It was back then, it is today.

What are we to think? Just two sides of the same coin. Why are we to assume the behavior of Black men and women today has not been passed down from slavery? Why not? Why not trace the evidence? Can we argue history is not repeating itself? From the first slaves to arrive on these shores, we are what has been beaten into us. We are what we have been conditioned to accept. What we have seen, what we have heard, how we have been treated. Every Black cannot shrug this off.

How long is the evolutionary process to overcome the DNA of slavery? It doesn't wash off with soap and water. Get erased with the reading of a book or two, the taking down of confederate statues, renaming of streets. Fade with the passing of time. Scrape the surface. Put the back against the wall. See what you find.

The Black Boy

So a Black boy is supposed to watch all this unfold and what? Watch his mother struggle to survive all alone. Watch his mother live out somebody's hand. Watch his mother struggle with an addiction, skip out on rent, hop from man to man, from woman to woman. Watch his father run off, abandon his family. Live without a father, without a father's influence, guidance, then be expected to come out as somebody else, somebody from a Black History Month calendar. Told, 'just keep your head up, just hold on.' For what?

So he's not supposed to act up. Not pick up a gun. Not pick up a drug habit. Just live at or below the poverty level and be okay with it. Not want to ride in a nice car, wear nice threads. Not question, why he came into this world. Not be upset. Not harbor ill-will towards everybody. Not give a fuck about anybody, not even himself. Just chill with it!

I hear what you say America. If he would just work hard. Study hard. He could have all those things and more. Even with all the trap doors in the way, he can pull it off. He can make it if he tries. No sir. A Black boy on Black Man Island is going to do what he believes he must do. There is no right or wrong. It's just the way it is. He's going to throw back what life gave him right back in its face.

Forget about what happened with the signing of the Emancipation Proclamation. That was just a pretty ceremony, a few breadcrumbs spread across the water. A rush of jubilation, it worked for a while, a brief moment. But like snow melting in the sun, Black men and women are who they are just below the surface. History for Black America began in 1619 in slavery. There are no king and queen ancestors to celebrate that history. It's mostly a harsh history of struggle. And everyone can't shake the past, they're just not that strong, not gifted enough. Truth is for Black folks on Black Man Island, our history is just a shade past slavery.

The Crumbling Neighborhoods

The Black community was once a beautiful thing. It truly was a village. Everyone knew you, who's child you were. Neighborhoods consisted of families, relatives, close friends, extended family. They were close knit neighborhoods.

Children were insulated, protected. If need be, chastised in their neighborhoods, by their adult neighbors. If you were acting up, whatever you were seen doing would beat you home. Neighbor up the street see girls twitching along were quick to call mom and give up the goods. Girls were quick to pull down skirts before they got home. Boys talking loud, cursing, talking tough, disrespecting their elders were quick to get chastised when they got home. There was discipline in the home. Established lines you could not cross as children.

Kids come home early from school, no problem. You go by Miss So And So house and wait there until mom gets home. She watched over you, fed you. Watched you do your homework before you went out to play. Who can you trust with your kids today? Who has the time, wants to be bothered with your kids?

At school, back in the day the principal, coaches would not allow students to act up. At church, the pastor gave strict instructions that had to be followed. The deacons, deaconesses would not allow kids to cut up in church. The eyes of the neighborhood were everywhere, for protection, guidance.

Gone are those close-knit neighborhoods and with them a priceless asset, the gift of encouragement. Neighbors and friends of the family asked kids about grades. Some gave a dollar for an A, fifty cents for a B. They kept telling kids they could do better. Admonished them if they failed to get up, 'dust yourself off and try again.'

Back in the day the teachers were mentors, they encouraged kids, 'try harder, you can do it, just don't quit.' Worked after school with kids. Kids looked up to their teachers. Today most teachers seem disconnected, there is little encouragement. It's not part of the curriculum. Teachers are not rated for encouragement.

Folks walked everywhere. You walked to the store. You walked to school. You walked to church. You pretty much walked wherever you had to go. It was safe back then. You could send your children on errands and not fear them getting robbed, kidnapped or worse gunned down for being in the wrong place at the wrong time.

Today the neighborhood is frightened of our kids, doors are locked, no encouragement. Neighbors dare not call a parent about a child. The reply may not be a thank you but a beat down or worse. What happened to the neighborhood? It's as if it was built on quicksand. In short, what building can remain standing or rather how long can a building remain standing when built on a crumbling foundation?

One glaring problem in the inner city Black community, we rely on a support system that is not sustainable. We all know what a pyramid is. A structure wide at the bottom that narrows as it rises to the top. The pyramids of Africa have survived centuries while other structures have tumbled. Why? It's simple, the foundation is broad, able to easily withstand the load as the structure narrows as it gets higher. The load at the very top is light.

Now if you turn the pyramid upside down, it won't work. It'll topple over. The weight at the top will be too great, there would be imbalance, the weight misplaced. The narrow point now at the bottom will not support the pyramid structure, it will simply topple over. That's today's inner city Black communities and neighborhoods.

The original neighborhood included a firm bottom foundation of upper income folks, working professionals, business folks. They are now long gone. They flew out as soon as they could. The Black hard-working middle class slowly erodes. Tired of struggling, holding on, unable to hold things together, they move out first chance. They want what everyone else wants, security, better schools, a better quality of life.

The result, the new base is a small minority trying to support the entire neighborhood. Those that remain consist of a small percentage of the borderline middle class. Perhaps the elderly, those trapped by limited income and no family. Perhaps some folks that inherited property remain. These folks intersect in the community and struggle to hold it together. This fragile foundation is overburdened with higher taxes, fees and still they receive less in services.

In our eroding Black communities, the majority in the middle of the pyramid are lower income Blacks and working poor. Most are stuck, unable to put the funds together to get out. Those that can are exiting by any means necessary.

The majority at the top of the pyramid are the impoverished, Blacks on the system, the criminal element, those stuck with bad habits. Some activists fight to hang on, refuse to leave the old neighborhood. They fight to preserve the Black community, the heritage. They fight to reduce drugs in the community. Often, they are targeted, forced out or worse murdered by the criminal element they fight against. No, the inverted pyramid system won't work, the strain on the foundation becomes too great. The result is a neighborhood ripe for gentrification or demise.

Everything heads south, not south to Miami but south in condition. The majority of housing falls into disrepair. The neighborhood crowds with renters. At that point, even the Section 8 tenants want out. Renters that remain don't give a damn and are not concerned with the declining tide. Long standing Black owned business are long shuttered. There is no clientele to support them. Schools are labeled failures. No gainful employment is available. Crime is on the upswing, drug abuse is rampant. The pyramid tumbles over and the result is a Black Man Island, something just short of a sharecropper's plantation.

The neighborhood crumbles. The neighborhood dies. Government money comes in, but it's misspent. No one is minding the mint. Politicians and their cronies steal and pilfer. A government dollar given for support, by the time it gets to the community is a dime and what can a dime do when a dollar wouldn't be enough.

Add it all up. The Black community is in real serious trouble, heading for the rim of the cliff. Worse, there appears no MLK, no Malcolm to guide Black America, steer it clear the fate of going over. The only question remaining, how can the inner cities of Black America survive? We are dead last in so many categories and in some categories, it's not even close.

A Crumbling Rock

There was a time when God was important in the Black community. The church was thought to be the cornerstone of the Black community. The church reverend was a leader, a pillar in the Black community. The reverend was a spokesperson for the Black community. The church leader was on the front line of defense against injustice.

The church was a backbone in the community. When there was a problem in the Black community, folks turned to the church. The church worked to defuse problems. The church was a welcome help in times of need. The church helped with bills, helped put food on the table, tide families over, kept marriages intact.

From the very beginnings of the civil rights movement, the church was a go between for the whites in power and Blacks in the community. Church leaders prayed for the people, strengthened, energized the people with a word.

During the civil rights movement, church leaders walked arm in arm with Dr. King. Strong Black leaders from around the country came up through the church. The church kept the Black community's eyes on the prize in the struggle for 'equal rights under the law.'

Dr. King got Blacks as far as he could, even to the point of paying with his blood. The ball was handed off and it seems to have been fumbled. What has happened to the Black Church?

There appears a lack of importance of the church in the Black community. A growing void, with no coherent messaging emanating from religious leaders in the Black community. One wonders, do church leaders talk, discuss needs regards the Black community? Or do they talk about stuff? Check out my new jet, my new house, my new car, my new cathedral, my new first lady.

The Black community used to fear God, God was our rock, our strength but today, one has to ask, where is God in our struggles? There is a growing disconnect between young Blacks and the church. Or is it a disconnect with the church leaders?

We might ask ourselves, which of the nationally known Black preachers would you follow? Outside of their own church's congregation, what is their national clout to lead Black America? Which preacher is ready and willing to forsake the roost of their church's altar for the greater good of Black America?

Which preacher is unafraid to speak the truth to the powers that be, to the people? Preachers today appear to behave like politicians, always politically correct. Are not say the wrong thing and get repudiated, banished by the press, even the president.

The Black community has great need of national leaders. Why hasn't another emerged from the church? If you study the Bible, in times of need God would send a leader, a Moses, a David, an MLK. The righteous was never forsaken. But today, there appears a disconnect from the church and political needs of the people, as if something must be protected. What is the church protecting?

We look at the protest marches and the absence of a prominent national preacher on the front line is visibly noticeable. Why is the church no longer at the forefront of political change for Black America? Why doesn't the protest march start at the church house with prayer? What is the preacher protecting or hiding from?

Once a pillar of the community, the church has been slowly eroding in significance. Is there growing unbelief in God or in the man of God? What have Blacks to lean on? When bad things happen, the non-believers will justify non-belief, "see if God was real, He would not have allowed that to happen." Why not? Why would it work that way, see God, then believe in God? The church is mostly silent. What happened to the Black church? What happened to the visionaries, the dreamers in the Black Church? Did dreams die when Dr. King died?

I often wonder. If Jesus landed on this planet and set foot in these United States, which church would he visit first? Which cathedral or mega church would he step into first? Would he set foot in a Catholic church or a Baptist church first? What preacher would he call first? Or would Jesus bypass the church altogether? Set up church on the street corners of the inner city.

Young Blacks are not blind, they can see. Where is the church in the struggle? It appears success in the Black church is more of one-upmanship. Come see what I got, not what I done. Once the pillar of the Black community, now just another part of a weakened and crumbling foundation. Closer to part of the problem than the solution.

THE MIS EDUCATION OF BLACK AMERICA

As one might imagine, right out of slavery the Black family's chief concern was eating, surviving. Kids had to help with chores, work the fields, get a job. Then again there were no schools for most ex-slaves. Schools for Blacks in America was an afterthought. Educating a Black child was of no importance, particularly in the segregated Jim Crow South.

Gradually Blacks began to stress getting a good education, study, work hard in school. Education was deemed of the utmost importance, the key to a better life, getting off that plantation. After years of struggling for better schools, Blacks received good news. In the 1954 case Brown v. The School Board of Education of Topeka, the supreme court ruled that segregation in public schools was illegal. Even if the schools were deemed equal, which they weren't.

Our ancestors had indeed fought hard for the proper education of Black children. But today, if we look at many of our public schools in the inner city, one might question whether education is important. If our schools are equal, then why are so many schools in the Black community deemed failing? If that's not the case, why do parents fight to send their kids to the best public schools. Or on the other hand, sacrifice and spend thousands to send their kids to private schools? Will move out of the inner city specifically to find better schools.

In many failing inner city public schools, students graduating high school are close to functionally illiterate. They can barely fill out a job application. So who's going to hire them? What is their future?

Rather than leave high school with the asset of a diploma, students leave high school with boots reshod with heavier lead on their feet. In a race that is a sprint, where are they expected to finish? What's really going on with the education of Black kids today?

The irony, Blacks are still told education is key to getting a good job, a better life. Does it matter? Black unemployment has always remained the highest in country. Economic opportunity for inner city Black youth remains scarce. The unemployment numbers for Black youth stays in the double digits regardless of how well the economy is doing.

Inevitably conversations arise questioning whether the old way was better. Suggesting that prior to the end of segregation, 'we had some great colored schools.' We had some 'good colored teachers.'

It was a grand plan, integrate schools. Send our kids to the better white schools. That will solve all our problems. Guess what, after forty plus years our inner city schools are still integrated and our kids are not getting an adequate education.

Are the powers that be paying attention? Is anyone looking at the elementary and middle schools? The failure of Black students doesn't mysteriously occur when they get to high school. At a time when a difference must be made in a child's life, the system appears to fail them. Sends them on to high school woefully unprepared.

By the time kids reach high school their die is cast. Teachers label them hopeless and pass them along to get them out of their class, out of the school. Students are doing everything but learning. Students are on cell phones during class. Their heads are on their desks. They're talking during class as if the teacher really is not there. It's common to find fighting prevalent amongst students in our failing schools. The risk for school violence against teachers is prevalent.

What is the objective of our high schools? Once we thought they were to prepare our young people for the future, the real world. Today the powers that be choose to focus on test scores. There seems little motivation and no pressure for kids to do well in school, bring home good grades. What good is a high school diploma if the student is not prepared for the real world? What has society done?

Are students sent to school to find the next sports superstar? The student population is just window dressing. If that be the case, there is no need to learn anything. There is more interest by the community in how the local high school teams are doing in sports than academics. How is the star athlete doing, will he get the nod of an elite college program? There's something to brag on.

Is there a correlation between little or no education and the prison system? The percentage of Black men in jail is disproportionately skewered towards poorly or uneducated Blacks. If you can't get a job to take care of your family, what is a young Black man supposed to do? The options are limited. Flipping burgers won't cut it. Guess what, selling drugs is the number one option. That or working two jobs if they can be found. The other grim options are the graveyard or jail. If schools do not exist to educate, why do schools exist? Do they exist to sell drugs, train up the next dope dealers? Provide a pipeline for the prison system?

Is there a correlation between lack of education in Black girls and teen pregnancy? We hear of Black girls with limited education competing with friends to become pregnant. The average age for pregnancy amongst Blacks remains lowest in the country. Chances are the father won't be there to support the child and mother. The number one option becomes, get on the system, welfare. Education is not important, not a requisite.

Teachers were once from the neighborhood school they grew up around. They were committed. Now we have many disinterested teachers imported from outside the neighborhood, working to get their student loans paid off. And yes, still our teachers are underpaid. By comparison pro athletes and entertainers are paid ungodly sums. And that's okay with society.

Who do we blame for our failed public schools in the Black community? The teachers appear to be fighting a losing battle. The list of problems is long. It's not apparent the students want to learn.

Teachers complain, today's parents don't discipline their kids, check homework. Kids come to school unprepared, unfed, dressed in the same clothes over and over. Parents won't show up for parent-teacher conference but they will show up at their kid's practice.

At the end of the day we must ask, why do we send our kids to schools that are failing? Do we send our kids to school to play sports, join the drill team, the band, the cheerleading squad, to get rid of them for a while, get them out the house?

What happens to the kids that don't make it to the pros? Colleges recruit young talent at an early age. Some starting in middle schools, coaches fighting over talent. Prestigious college coaches are known to offer kids still in middle school an athletic scholarship. What does that say about the system, when a notable college coach sends a letter to a kid in middle school? Why would the parent or the child concern themselves with education?

How many kids that dreamed the dream ever make it? What happens when the dream doesn't pan out? Does anyone care? What happens to the thousands of boys that don't make it each year? What happens after draft day? They are prima donnas their entire life. Coddled by all, the parents, the teachers, the coaches, classmates, the fans. Draft day is over and their life is in pieces, no more accolades, nothing. The cold cruel world is waiting. They did nothing in school, so they know nothing. Is there PTSD aid for high school and college athletes?

When kids leave failing public schools, where are these children headed? The majority of students leaving our failing inner city public high schools are not prepared for work, unless we include McDonalds or some other minimum wage job. They are not prepared to succeed in college. Is there any effort to turn the tide?

On occasion we hear of a successful public school or school district, in New York, in Chicago, in Los Angeles, wherever. Some sponsored by pro athletes, others organized by well-intentioned community leaders. They are few and far between. America seems unwilling or unable to duplicate successful schools nationwide. Why is that?

Is it a money thing? The government forces our kids to go to school to the benefit of political hacks and cronies. Follow the money. Per child, how much is spent on a high school education? According to some national education stats, on average, it costs anywhere from $10-$16,000 per year per student to send a child to public school. Are we getting close to our money's worth? Why not just keep them at home, give the money to the students, it makes no sense? Yet America continues to fund this broken public school system in the inner city.

Follow the money, if the bulk is not going to the teachers or the students, where is it going? What value do we place on inner city kids? That we would send them into the world upon graduating, not educated but crippled with a public school diploma. Once education was an important pillar of the Black community. Today what can we call getting an education in the inner city? What does it mean? What is its value?

The Neighborhood Black Business

Once upon a time there were respected Black owned businesses in our Black neighborhoods. Black communities teemed with Black businesses. For one thing, Blacks were not allowed to set foot in so-called white businesses, at least not through the front door. Black doctors and dentists had offices in the community. Blacks owned commercial property, small motels, funeral homes, restaurants, corner bars, fashionable night clubs, small office buildings, not to mention the barbershop and the hair salon.

When Blacks couldn't shop across town, they didn't have a choice but to buy Black. Blacks built their own economy in their nearby neighborhoods. They didn't have to go across town to shop where they weren't wanted, not allowed. Before it was burned down in 1921, Tulsa's Black Wall Street was a shining example of what Blacks could do in business. The sky was the limit. Now we are left to ask, what happened to our neighborhood Black owned businesses?

You would think all these businesses became obsolete or just altogether left the community for no good reason. Oh but no, once the white establishments allowed Blacks to shop, it was if they were giving something away. Blacks flocked to these so called white owned businesses. They watched us like hawks, took our money but still did not let Blacks try on clothing.

Most Black-owned businesses that have remained in the community are perceived as mandatory Black, the funeral home, barber and hair salon. Outsiders either can't do or won't do. The remainder of most other businesses are owned by foreigners. Do these foreigners support the community where they exist? Do they even give a damn about the neighborhood? Are they held accountable?

Within the Black community Blacks once had working trades. What happened to Black construction trades, the carpenters, painters, roofers, concrete workers, plumbers, electricians, builders. Blacks took their sons to work, passed that trade down. Now those jobs have been taken over by mostly Hispanic workers. Blacks are all but left out in the cold. No longer do Blacks build much of anything.

Even the house cleaning jobs, the housekeeping hotel jobs that were once a mainstay for the Black female population are gone. Taken over by foreigners. What's left? Blacks struggle to hold on to retail jobs, landscaping jobs, cutting grass, repairing flats, washing cars.

Still Blacks are an economic force in this country. The buying power of Black America is projected to exceed 1 trillion dollars annually. What does that mean? Not much, for the most part Blacks are the piggybank of the big box stores such as Walmart and the foreign owned corner stores. What would they be without Black buyers? The sad tale, loss of Black owned businesses in the Black community is a loss of investment in the community. The money Blacks spend leaves the community, never to return.

What do you see? Does it make any sense? The stranglehold tightens and it seems to be working. Our communities continue to struggle and are dying. Why isn't business being taught in high school? How to start a business? How to fund a business? How to succeed in business? Blacks open a business and must figure it out along the way. And when they fail there is no bailout. Once pillars of the community, Black businesses in the inner city are for the most part, like dinosaurs. They don't exist.

THE UN-HEALTH OF BLACK AMERICA

Were Blacks better off when they took care of their sick with homemade remedies? Today take a look around the inner city Black community. Why are there so many clinics and not doctor offices in or nearby our Black communities? Medical clinics, dialysis clinics, blood plasma clinics, drug stores dot the landscape. What's getting us sick? Is there a conspiracy, to keep us sick in order to make money? That would not be a surprise.

When Blacks see the doctor there is no bedside manners concern, to know the patient. For the most part, it's a five minute visit and take two pills and don't call me. Blacks appear often overprescribed for drugs, guinea pigs to drug manufacturers and the doctors that profit off them. Poor Blacks, the elderly Blacks must often decide whether to eat or pay for drugs, debate whether to keep the utilities on, pay rent. All the while, politicians sit on their hands.

Blacks are mostly fearful of going to the hospital and for good reason. A quick diagnosis or rather the misdiagnosis can kill you. If not, the hospital bill surely will. Poor Blacks are often sent home quickly before they are healed or after being improperly diagnosed, another possible death sentence. The politicians sit on their hands.

On the other street corners of the neighborhood we find some of the culprits. Drugs are readily available but they don't come with warnings on labels. Any illegal drug so desired is readily available. Drug abuse is prevalent in the Black community, with little means of prevention and no 'just say no programs.' Availability is not just that of weed, crack and heroin but now opioids are at the forefront. Drugs are everywhere, creating more problems, taking an immeasurable toll on the community. Why, how is this happening? Blacks don't manufacture drugs. All the while, politicians sit on their hands.

On the other corners we find the corner stores we frequent and what are they selling? These corner stores sell cigarettes by the carton or by the single. They sell the cheapest liquor, rot gut liquor. They sell us fried, greasy food with little regard to how healthy the food is. Is anyone monitoring the food preparation in these corner stores?

Do you think Walmart gives a damn about the amount of junk food Blacks buy for themselves, their kids? The government certainly does not care. It's so easy to talk about eating healthy when you have money to eat the best. Hire a cook to cook healthy, use all the right foods and ingredients. But how is a family of four going to eat healthy on minimum wage and low-income jobs? How can they avoid the 'four for four dollars' value meals at the fast food joints? Does the fast food industry really care how healthy their meals are?

Blacks are at the head of so many lists, diabetes, high blood pressure, heart disease, sickle cell. The life span of a Black man is approximately 69 years if they're lucky. The life span of a white man is approximately 76 years. Why is the Black man's life span less? Is it because it's valued less? Don't sell us it's a Black man thing.

What about mental health disorders, is anyone concerned? Mentally impaired Blacks are more apt to wander and reside on the city streets than the beds of a hospital. They are more apt to be locked up in a jail cell than a mental institution. They are mostly treated as the disposable and the lack of their proper treatment is given little thought by the government. The politicians sit on their hands.

Can the spread of sexually transmitted disease in the Black community get any worse? We are the leaders of the pack in the contraction of STDs. What is being done by the government to stop the spread in of STDs in our communities? Abstinence, just say is not an option. Is there still an ongoing Tuskegee Experiment in the Black Community? We wouldn't know, the politicians sit on their hands.

And now comes the coronavirus pandemic. Covid-19 is killing a disproportionate number of Blacks. The outcries of why are loud. But the mystery is easily solved, just look to treatment of Blacks as a whole. We are last and losing ground. The un-health of Black America seems all but a piggy bank for drug manufacturers, doctors, clinics, hospitals and America seems disinterested to change a thing. Healthcare was never a pillar in the Black community. Covid-19 has made it plain and the politicians sit on their hands.

The Poli-tricks of Black America

Why did our Black ancestors want the vote? Was it validation for equality? The fifteenth amendment gave Blacks the right to vote in 1870. However southern states stopped Blacks at the polls with election laws such as the poll tax and the literacy test. Today we don't have that problem but how many Blacks vote come election day? Sadly we are last in that category too.

Why is it that we have to have racism on the ballot to get Blacks to vote, to motivate us to go out to the polls? Why is it that we have to hear the racist dog whistles to be motivated to vote? It's as if Blacks still haven't figured out the power of the vote, elections have consequences.

In the early going, no one thought our vote would change a damn thing. Yet today Black politicians are in charge of countless cities and communities. We have Black elected officials on the state and the national level. Still the Black populace represented by those politicians are mired in stagnation, in some cases going backwards.

Our Black leaders from the civil rights era are slowly dying off. Where do we look for leadership? We have hundreds of Black politicians, thousands of Black elected officials today. Can we expect or look for the next great Black leader to come from the current political field? They appear mired in popularity contests. They can't or won't rock the boat if they want to get elected or so they seem to believe. They appear one dimensional. Solidly behind the fight against racism but they test the wind to decide if they should speak up on anything else, let alone ruffle feathers. How else can one explain conditions of the inner city?

What would have happened had MLK chosen political correctness in his dealings with the then president, the white establishment. They told him the timing wasn't right, he should wait. MLK even faced criticism from Black leaders. Some said he was an Uncle Tom, others believed he was too aggressive. Why is it that our leaders have to be so politically correct today? On the other hand, why should they come out of their comfort zone to champion a call for reparations, a Black agenda?

Today we must ask, what is the Black agenda? If you consider yourself even somewhat educated, somewhat on top of current events. If the man from the moon showed up on your doorstep and asked you the question, what would you tell him? Blacks have countless problems. You might blurt out, the 'Black lives matter' narrative. Followed by a shout, "police brutality must stop."

Someone might shout lack of education because our schools appear woefully inadequate. Someone could shout, jobs, we need better paying jobs. Throw in the racist justice system needs change. But all these appear symptoms of a greater problem.

Put the patient on the operating table. He's dying. Does it matter if we open him up? We can't do him any worse. It might just save his life. We have to determine what's making him sick but we stop short. Have we become that insignificant, even to ourselves? Are our politicians fearful of rocking the establishment? If we don't stand for something, we'll fall for anything. Does it matter?

Our ancestors fought and died for the right to vote. We went in droves to the polls and voted for Clinton and Obama. That was like voting for our boys. Somebody we knew personally. It was personal. Yet there was no Black agenda on either's platform. Today, Black elected officials are in charge of many cities but we are unable to change a damn thing. We celebrate the minor and pigeonhole the major.

We once had Black leaders that were 'called' to lead, not hold offices or positions of popularity. Martin Luther King, Jr, Malcom X, Fred Hampton, Medgar Evers, Fannie Lou Hamer, they were born to do this, to uplift their people. It was their fate. They woke up and went to bed with the Black Agenda on their mind each and every day. Today the fear is our Black leaders are no threat. Why? Who amongst today's Black leaders is next in line to press the Black Agenda ad nauseum?

The accountant says, numbers don't lie. One and one equals two, today, yesterday and tomorrow. Here in 2020, the inner cities of Black America are in turmoil. Years and years of Black control but if you drive through the Black sections of the inner city, you will get a dose of reality. It appears all that has been achieved is accentuation of the negative. Drugs are rampant. Crime is rampant. Education is sparse. Sexually transmitted diseases are rampant. Affordable housing is sparse. Jobs are scarce. Addictions are evident. Single women heading households is the norm.

Our political mouthpieces bang the drum like we're really involved, we're into it man. If so, then why are the facts what they are? Inquiring minds want to know. Do you see any change on the horizon, for the Black inner city household? If you live in a city that has Black leadership at the top, do you see a 'change gonna come' revival for the Black community? How long have Blacks maintained control in certain cities? How much longer do we need control? Can we afford the wait? The ship is taking on water. And we're shuffling chairs on the Titanic. Not realizing the ship is going down.

The plight of the African American in America is well documented. In 2020, what do you see changing? You got a few more rich Blacks, some super rich Blacks. Some that get twenty million dollars a year or more to act, play a song, hit a ball, play basketball, football but what's changing back home in the old neighborhoods? The rich take a few family and friends along for the ride but unfortunately, the masses are left behind.

Speaking plainly, what is the Black agenda? The great fear is not the white nationalists, nor the racist cops. The greatest fear is the fixed apathy in our own inner city neighborhoods. Black brothers, the predators fighting over that same bone, the scraps off master's table. Unable to see clearly, feeling their way in the dark, shoot first, take what you can. Can a brother feed his family, without having to hurt somebody?

After our elections, the pundits and political analysts analyze the data and declare the difference in the election was unequivocally the Black vote. The pundits suggest the Black vote was the difference, they didn't go to the polls and that's why the republicans won. Or the Black turnout was higher than expected and decisively in favor of the democratic candidate. The Black leaders stand on stage and celebrate the victory with the candidates. Blacks in their living room celebrate. We won. What did we win?

Why are Blacks celebrating? What has changed, what will change? Are we to assume that because our candidate won, the needle will move in the Black community? Are we to assume that the boats of Black America will rise like the boats the white folk are in? if that be the case then why do Blacks remain in this predicament? We are last in unemployment, last in education and first in incarceration? And it's been that way for a while.

During the election cycle boatloads of money are pumped into the Black community. The premise, we need the Black vote. Must get the Black vote out. After the election money trickles in, if at all. Sadly, it would appear, the Black votes are more important than Black lives.

Is it a question of leadership? Black folk don't mind being led. It appears Black folk have a problem with accountability. We don't hold our Black politician's and democratic leader's feet to the fire. A politician can rob the community blind or watch it get robbed. Blacks will forgive them and vote for them again. Perhaps Donald Trump said it best, "I could shoot someone dead on 5th Avenue and not lose my supporters." Is that Black enough for you? It appears to be the sentiment of some Black politicians and for good reason.

Why do Blacks continue to drink the Kool Aid? We listen to the silver-tongued politicians, dressed in suits. They tell us what we want to hear. A chicken in every pot, a car in every driveway, free this, free that. They come in singing the same old song, Tweedledee and Tweedledum. And when they get in office, nothing. Where are the legislative victories for Blacks, the initiatives on justice reform, jobs, training, economic development, affordable housing? Every damn politician runs on change but nothing ever changes, the needle does not move.

If justice is blind, then why per capita are Blacks locked up in greater numbers, given longer sentences? How many Blacks are in jail because of crooked cops, crooked DA's, crooked judges. If you're Black in America, justice looks upon you differently, looks the other way if you're white. Justice is not blind, America is blind to the injustice.

Why is substandard housing the norm on Black Man Island? We all know home ownership is the backbone of a neighborhood. Yet the percentage of homeownership amongst Blacks when compared to whites and other ethnicities is least. The struggle is real. How can you pay rent, own a home when jobs are limited? When the income of a family is borderline, just barely above poverty or below? When the households are headed by single mothers with just one income, how is home ownership possible?

We hear a lot of political talk and that's all it is, about the improvement of the Black race, "African Americans." But it's mostly about the few, the small percentage, certain individuals and their accomplishments. They are the exception not the norm. For most Black Americans on the island, their eyes are not on the prize. A better life for their families appears a mirage. Their daily life is a grind, choosing to live for today, survive. If they can make it through another day, that's the prize.

It is indeed unfortunate. America does not tie, refuses to tie the ills of inner city Black America to slavery, sees no need for reparations. It is the reflection America refuses to look at, refuses to address in its totality. Answer this America, why are Blacks in this predicament? "Well see, Blacks always been lazy, naturally lazy. They just no good. They will steal you blind." The lies told about Blacks during slavery are the same lies spoken today. Who said it first, "if you tell a lie enough times, it will eventually be believed."

THE CRIME PROBLEM

Perhaps the biggest problem plaguing Black America is crime. The thorn in its side that won't go away but only seems to get worse. Some suggest the new plantation is prison, home to free labor. The ultimate Black Man Island, where escape is near impossible. The recidivism rate for Black men is over 50%. No doubt people are getting rich off incarceration. So you have to question whether America will ever address crime reduction in earnest.

The senseless killings

Does any killing make sense? Cold blooded murder that makes no sense. You look at a man's woman the wrong way, whatever that means and get killed. You disrespect a man by how you talk to him, how you look at him and get killed. You owe a friend some money and refuse to pay, you get killed. A dope dealer in an effort to protect his territory, kills rivals to send a message. Then there is retaliation, someone else gets murdered and another and another, most times not even the intended targets.

Innocent children gunned down in their living rooms, on their way to school, outside playing in their yards. Bystanders gunned down by wayward bullets, the unintended victims of our violent culture. And the Black community sits on their hands distracted. Ready to go to war over racist cops. But the blood is in our neighborhood's streets, is on our hands because we do little and demand nothing.

If you live in the inner city, most of us have been to the vigils, the funerals. We've listened to the anger. Watched the tears fall. Words, marches, vigils are never of themselves going to change this culture of violence. Preacher's words fall on deaf ears. The people that need to hear, don't want to hear it. To the brothers on the street, it does not appear there is another choice, no economic option. "Brothers ain't gonna work it out" are not willing to work it out.

What happened to 'stop the violence' movements? Every now and then the 'stop the violence' signs popped up. Maybe there was a march. The pastor is interviewed and preaches to the choir. Then the screen turns to black. The signs have no meaning, the preaching has no impact. There is not a prolonged outcry, just another funeral and passing tears.

The aftermath of the carnage, for the most part young Black men lie dead in the street. All that energy, all those dreams gone from the Black community, the world. Friends hold vigils. Parents are left dumbfounded. Mothers and children left despondent. No one seems to know anything, how it happened, why it happened, nothing, no answers, just questions. Add to the murders, the thousands of lives impacted by injuries, the medical care needed, the depression experienced.

We pray, ask, oh Lord why has thou forsaken us? But it appears we've forsaken God. We say we believe in the good Lord but if He stepped off the bus would we acknowledge Him? If the good Lord hung out with the thugs and forgotten people, would we disparage him? Question his veracity as a spiritual leader? Would we cross the street if He came our way? Would He get gunned down in the streets for asking why all the killing? Would He be run out of town for talking bad about the political injustice?

The top of the local and national news is constantly filled with crime. Disproportionately filled with Black faces. Faces that are getting younger and younger. What can you say when you hear on the news, a 13 year old, a 14 year old and maybe boys as young as 9 years of age are committing heinous crimes, for kicks, for no rhyme or reason. It's unexplainable? Seems they have no fear of consequences. Or are they just acting up, crying out for attention?

Drugs in the Black community

The dirty little secret part two, seems no one really cares about the plethora of drugs in the Black community. Care enough to march like 'Black Lives Matter.' Care enough to speak out against it. Care enough to look for solutions. We know it's about money, but do we care enough to solve the money problem in the Black community?

What is the real cost of illegal drugs in the Black community? We all know too well the daily shootings, the murders, the lengthy incarcerations but what about the cost to the Black family. Drugs and crime leave behind broken families, a father gone, a brother gone, a child left all alone, mothers crying. The emotional weight, how can we estimate that cost? A continuing generational cost, from father to son, to his son.

How do drugs get into the Black communities? We know for sure, Blacks don't manufacture drugs in the Black community. Cocaine, heroin are brought in from elsewhere. China sends us illegal drugs. Mexico sends us Oxycontin drugs. Drugs are prescribed by bogus doctors and sold in the Black community. But it's not enough to stop the flow of drugs into the community. The root cause is about economics, money, supply and demand. Victims of circumstance, what is a brother left to do? It's easy for someone to speak about a problem when it doesn't affect them. Brothers don't see a way out.

The Collateral Damage

No one wants to live next to the drug house. So there goes the block. Vacant and even occupied homes are vandalized. People work to rebuild a home, the neighborhood. The vandals vandalize and their work is thrown back in their face. Its humiliating, defeating. The reality, the murders are costly but so are the property crimes. Homes getting broken into, cars burglarized, carjackings, assaults, all to feed a drug habit, finance a lifestyle.

We look to place the blame. Is rap music the culprit? Does rap, hip hop owe the Black community anything? There is no debate as to the fact that hip hop has had an enormous impact on society. Listen to it every day. Get brainwashed. Could it be that it sells our youth a dream? But what would cleaned up lyrics sell for?

What would happen if rap artists were asked to start singing about positive Black messages? Would we hold them in less esteem? Doesn't matter, they won't change. That music wouldn't sell in the world of young whites that spend billions on wanting to be cool. Can you blame the artists for not changing? No, because the Blacks that need the message wouldn't buy it either. Niggas, bitches and hos, kill, kill, kill, fuck this, fuck that, sounds like slavery talk regurgitated. Not by the slave master but by slave descendants. We are still the same with different brands on our backs, designating who owns us. We have to get to the root causes.

The Numbers Don't Lie

Frequently Chicago makes the evening news, not to discuss the weather in the windy city but to list the number of people shot and killed on the streets. It reads like the casualties of a war zone.

According to FBI crime statistics, Chicago is one of America's deadliest cities. Yet it's not the deadliest city in America per capita. Per 100,000 the list of America's most deadliest cities follows a trail directly to cities with significant Black populations, countless cities, like Baltimore, Memphis, St. Louis, Atlanta, Detroit, Shreveport, New Orleans, Chicago, Miami, Birmingham. They all share significant Black populations and corresponding high crime, with high poverty rates amongst Blacks.

The blood is in the streets.

The Facts: According to the 2010 census data, the Black demographics of USA, puts the Black Population in the U.S. at 38.9 Million, or about 13.5% of total population. The population of Black Males in the U.S. is estimated at 18.8 Million, roughly 6.5%.

The Facts: According to recent FBI Crime Stats, the male population in prison is somewhere around 2,220,000. The number of Black Males in Prison is roughly 821,000(that's anywhere from 38-40% of all males in prison). What's up with that?

Facts: From the FBI files, 7,886 Blacks were killed in 2015. Black on Black murders: 97% of Blacks were killed by Blacks. How is this possible? Why?

The Unexplained Mysteries

The people look on perplexed. Asking why is this happening? The white man believes he knows the answer. "Blacks are arrested because a great number of them are just no good. It's there in Black and white. Blacks don't want to do right." Therefore, we should believe this is just a bad apple situation. There is a far greater number of bad apples in the Black race, than any other race in America. We all know there are a number of bad apples in all races. But we're talking about 38-40%.

Blacks on the other hand believe the numbers are a direct result of racism, the crooked, racist cops. Black men are victims of a corrupt judicial system. So Blacks march for an end to police brutality, judicial reforms. There is no question there are racist cops, racism in the criminal justice system does exist. But we're talking about 38-40%.

Look closely. Crime is a symptom. Follow along. You are born to a single mother, in poverty, in an impoverished neighborhood, a crime ridden neighborhood. This is what you see from day one and every day thereafter. You are sent to a failing school. And by the way, what would a failing school be expected to produce? Leave school. There are no opportunities, no good paying jobs, life is a daily struggle. And we scratch our heads at the end results.

Let's repeat this, Black males are 6.5% of the general population and 38-40% of the prison population. What are the Vegas odds any Black male will get off the plantation? What are the odds a person born into this plantation life will not end up in jail or dead? Black on Black crime is rampant throughout Black Man Islands in the U.S. of A. Multiply this form of cannibalizing, what do you get? A stranglehold upon Black America that no one seems interested in breaking. A cancer spreading with no rush to a cure.

But there is a larger question. Why does any white person end up in jail? White people are born with white privilege. The race starts and whites are put ahead by fifty yards in a hundred yard race. At the same time, Blacks have on lead boots. How is it that any whites end up in jail? Even if a white person is born into poverty, they are ahead of all the Blacks in the race. White people don't see this. They only know what the news reports on Blacks. But how many whites are never charged, never face conviction? If they do, their charges are lessened? Never gets put on their record.

Seems the mentality on Black Man Island is to just work hard, hustle and then die. Rather than support each other's efforts to escape, we are more apt to tear each other down. Rather we grab hold of our sisters and brothers dream and pull them back down, into the bucket, the abyss of nothing. Keep them on Black Man Island, rather see their neighbor's life as a train wreck than a success story.

Where did this mentality originate? America doesn't want to address the issue, refuses to address it. As if unwilling to look into the mirror, unwilling to get the doctor's prognosis. The patient is dying, doesn't have long to live. By ignoring the illness, it will go away.

Better yet, let the patient die. Become depressed and commit suicide, matricide, patricide, infanticide, another homicide. That seems to have been America's hope from day one. Black America says it has a cold, the flu and white America says take two pills and don't call back. Or as politicians like to do, just kick the can further down the road.

No, once again it must be expressed clearly, succinctly, the lingering effects of slavery are at the root cause of the Black man's proclivity to commit crimes, become a criminal. If the slave owner deprives the slave of basic necessities for a decent life, what is the slave left to do? Every Black man cannot be a Frederick Douglas. Slavery ain't that far removed from a Black man or woman on Black Man Island. The environment has not changed, just the date. That plantation existence, struggle keeps oozing to the surface.

PART IV. THE BAND AID

THE CRUTCH SYSTEM

If you keep someone in need, you own them and they can name themselves if they so please. Makes no difference. Is it a conspiracy by the government to create programs that on the surface are meant to help Blacks but in reality, are nothing more than a trap? Nothing more than a crutch to intoxicate them, keep them dependent.

Look around, have Black inner city communities gone stagnant, backwards? Are they content to satisfy themselves with the scraps off the master's table? Are we to ignore all the successes Blacks have made as an anomaly? Rather just write off the masses of Black people who can't seem to find success. Ignore all the opportunities in this country, just allow the Black masses to remain enamored with a get over mentality?

The Economics

We know well the quandary for low income Black families. Few if any can find the good paying jobs, that don't require a college education, specialized training. The money low income Blacks do earn, where is it spent? For the most part it's spent to survive. The money is spent on perishables. Very little, if any money remains. Therefore, is there any thought given to savings, financial planning, the stock market? Anything saved to go towards home ownership, a college fund? It's easier to just throw up both your hands.

Blacks are an economic engine for retail juggernauts. So why would big box stores, the corner stores want to see things change in the Black Community? They make tons of money off the plight of poor Blacks. It's so easy to say America has too many people on welfare. But where is the push to end welfare, eliminate why it exists. Determine what are the other options? These retailers appear nothing more than sharecropper's stores. Give them the money with one hand and take it back with the other.

What is the system?

The system is the Black people's attempt to make something out of nothing. Forget about the American Dream, after all, it's just a dream. To live life as best they can, by any means necessary. The system is waiting for a handout and not a hand up, from the government, from anyone. Looking for loopholes in the law, breaking the law to live and not flourish.

Taxes

Don't pay taxes, it's easier to cheat.

If you have a business, a hustle, you simply don't file a tax return. Owners of small businesses such as the corner store, hair salon, barber shop, the babysitter, house sitter, elderly sitter pay little if any in taxes. Self-contractors, such as plumbers, electricians, roofers, lawncare providers, resellers, recyclers choose to under pay or don't pay taxes. If a business is paid in cash or personal checks its easy. Some businesses and individuals will only accept cash for their services. Paying taxes is not even given a second thought.

Bottom line, if you don't pay Uncle Sam you are saving money. Why should struggling Black folks pay taxes? Don't forget, Blacks didn't invent this. It's commonly believed that the rich don't pay any or nearly enough in taxes. So the thinking of the everyday Black(as learned from the white man) is to avoid paying taxes. To survive, Blacks must take advantage of the system.

Earned Income Tax Refund

You see the advertising every first of the year, "get thousands in tax refunds." Tax preparers advertise as much as accident lawyers. It sounds too good to be true but it's real, courtesy of Uncle Sam. In short, it pays to have a kid or two and barely work or only work a little to qualify for the max in earned income and tax credits. And by the way it pays to be 'head of the household' as opposed to married with kids filing joint.

Individuals works retail or fast food. They are not earning much. But should they work all the overtime available or work to advance themselves? Why should they? When it pays to work fewer hours, fewer months, remain entrenched on a low income job. Why work long hours, take more abuse from a low paying job, a thankless job? You work the system to your advantage. An individual with three kids can get a refund of as much as $10,000 or more in earned income and tax credits. Don't tell me Black people are lazy. It pays to work the system, not work.

Assistance Programs

Are entitlement programs what our ancestors were fighting for, food stamps, the free phone program, section 8 housing programs, disability checks? It seems it pays for women, not just Black women to get pregnant, have a kid or two or three, then get on the system. Who can argue with free rent, free medical care, free food, a check in the mail every month?

Add getting in line for anything that's free, the toy giveaway at Christmas, the turkey giveaway at Thanksgiving, the utility bill payment program, the free food pantry. Stand in line all day and complain but it's best you don't get out of line unless you have a stand in. You'll lose your spot. It's intoxicating, the wait is justifiable.

A woman while on the system, gets a boyfriend, slash side husband. Let him live with you while you're on public assistance. He's not on the lease but he helps with the bills, sometimes. The landlord says nothing cause he's only worried about getting his money. Besides, he knows how hard it is out there.

Government Programs, are they meant to help or hurt? Can the recipients be weaned off? Do they care to be weaned off? The government promotes being single. Living single is a better way of life. Remember, roughly 70% of Black households are headed by a single woman. The system was made for them. You come out ahead if you're single with children on the tax form, on the application for aid, the giveaway programs.

The sad truth, our politicians fight for and consider it a great victory if the federal money spent on entitlements is increased. In effect, they're thinking, the promoting of more government reliance is what is needed. It's an easy political victory, a layup. Remember, if you can get them to need you, you own them and their vote, what difference is there to what name they call themselves?

Add up all the entitlements, what has changed in the Black Community? Are they a help or a harm? If you can get someone to need you, rely on you, you own them. That's the system operating in the inner city Black community. What is America perpetuating? A new kind of slavery or maybe the same old slavery. Inner city Black America is a slave to the system. If not, has dependence on the system gone up or down for Blacks since inception?

It appears Blacks are conditioned to continue relying on government subsidies. How will it be possible for Blacks to escape the Black Man Islands of this country? Look back over the years, has government subsidies changed Black American communities for the better, regardless of the political party in charge? Most everyone goes through hard times at one point or another but when it becomes a lifestyle, it becomes a trap with no escape.

What does entitlements sound like? "I am entitled to free stuff. I deserve free stuff." Entitlements are the government's attempt to forego needed surgery by placing a band aid over the wounds of slavery. Entitlements are like pouring half of what's needed and rather than help the situation, the situation is made worse. If America wanted to help poor people, the disadvantaged, it would not put crutches under able bodied Black Americans. Rather America would teach them to fish. Put fish in their ponds. Why hide the cancer with a band aid, keep telling the patient you'll be fine?

The Lawsuit Culture

Why are Blacks inundated with the lawyer's ads? 24-7, it's 'need a check, get in a wreck', 'slip and fall, give me a call.' Everywhere you look there's a billboard advertising, 'get yourself a lawsuit.' Every time you turn on the tv, there's a lawyer advertising of accident injury. It becomes subliminal. Not if but get yourself into an accident.

There are the professional accident hounds who turn work into search for an accident. The local cab driver has multiple car accidents while working. We complain about their driving. Seems they are not just driving bad, they are seeking out accidents. Professional accident hounds will tell you If it's raining, "I gotta go to work, its raining, I know I can catch me a lawsuit."

This is not a white or Black problem. It just seems Blacks are bombarded by countless ads on tv, prompting one and all to get in on the class action lawsuits, for asbestos, cancer causing products or agents(seems everything causes cancer), toxic spills, prescription drugs. The best part, no money up front is required. What do these ads promote? Why work when you can get a lawsuit. Just throw up both your hands, work the system.

Repeated advertising subliminally promotes a culture of getting over. How could it not? This is not a knock on legitimate accident injuries. But how many times have you been frustrated by a tap on the bumper that turns into a major accident? All this does is feed the narrative of 'get over mentality'. Why work when you can catch an accident or lawsuit, frivolous or not. Will this change? No, the lawyers write the laws. Over 50% of those in Congress have law degrees. Would they take a pay cut? Ask their lawyer friends to take a pay cut?

<u>Drugs</u>

Of course illegal drugs are prevalent in the hood but let's talk about the prescription drug hustle. Simply put, patients obtain prescription drugs through bogus illnesses then turn around and sell the drugs. You have unscrupulous doctors that are running nothing more than pill mills. Opportunistic dealers, a nephew, a grandson turns around and sells grandma's pain pills, splits the profit with grandma. Get a pill for free and sell it for ten dollars. It's easy money, no repackaging, no cooking, no mixing.

Seems that no one cares, drugs still kill. Politicians sit on their hands, doesn't seem important enough. Seems as long as it mostly effects the expendable, it's okay. The drug manufacturers are one of the most powerful lobbyist groups. Follow the money.

Theft

Thieves, employees steal from the big box stores, Home Depot, Walmart, other national retailers, even from the mom and pop operators. Steal from their neighbor while they're at work. Put the word out, thieves steal on demand. Thieves can get you whatever you need in car parts. All that's needed is the year, make and model. You'll have the part the next day.

The latest fashions, you can get them before they hit the street. This is the get over culture of Black Man Island, to find a way, make a way, to live better. If society does not care about the improvement of Black Man Island, then Blacks adapt.

The Hustle Jobs

Every week the government puts out a report on unemployment in the country. You don't need the report to judge unemployment in the hood. Take a stroll through the Black community. Black men are on street corners, in parks and playgrounds. On sidewalks, playing dominos, checkers, chess, drinking liquor, smoking blunts, shooting the breeze.

What do these men do when they need a dollar? They hustle, beg on the corner. Put in a half days work wherever. Illegal gambling is alive, the dice game, the all-night card games, illegal sports betting, the con game. They get money from mom's purse, from the longtime girlfriend. Sell the food stamps. Put the utility bill in their name for a few dollars. Use their identity as a dependent on income taxes for a few dollars. What does illegal have to do with it? It's called survival.

Predatory Lending

The scourge of the Black community is credit offered by Pay Day loans, the local pawn shop, the loan shark. Blacks are quickly turned down by traditional lenders then turn to these unscrupulous lenders. Some have interest rates well above 100%. The borrower never pays off these loans.

Yet why is there no noise regarding predatory lending, no outcry? Predatory lending is nothing more than an extenuation of 'sharecropper' lending. Politicians sit on their hands, seems there is nothing that can be done to outlaw this scourge. Why Lord? It makes no sense or does it. Follow the money.

Scraping the Bottom

Is life on Black Man Island any different from the plight of a slave, the sharecropper. Reach it to them with one hand and take it back with the other hand. Connect the dots, today the slavery system exists. Those that can sing and dance, jump, have a special skill can earn their freedom. The rest are left to fight for the scraps off master's table. After all the dots are connected, a picture forms. It's clear. Black Man Island is just another name for the plantation.

Willie Lynch said if you want to create a permanent, a subservient nigger, scare the nigger into eating out your hand, have them depend on the slave master for everything. Take the biggest buck on the plantation, strip him naked. Tie his limbs to two powerful horses, then beat the hell out of those horses. Thereby splitting the buck in two, mind you all this in front of the slaves, men, women and children. Then master asks, "who's next?"

Every Black cannot be a Frederick Douglas. We celebrate Frederick Douglas, and rightly so. But what about all the Black men that couldn't escape from old master. Total it all up, what do we have? Is anyone talking seriously about lasting change. This system of dependence appears permanent. There appears to be great profit in poverty.

There is no mystery to the why a large percentage of Blacks stay on some aspect of the system for life, down on their perpetual bad luck? Government assistance was once thought of as a temporary fix. This 'get over' culture is nothing more than a throwback to slavery. A perpetuation of old master's perception of slaves, "they're lazy, they don't want to work, they'll steal you blind. Just too dumb to make it on their own." If you tell a lie enough times, it gets believed. Even by those the lie is told on. If you can get them to need you, you own them. Who cares what name they go by? This is when the preacher poses, "it's mighty quiet up in here saints."

PART V. THE DEMOCRATIC QUANDARY

THE BIG DISTRACTION

Everywhere you go, Blacks are talking about Donald Trump. He's no Barack Obama. He's dumb, an idiot. He's destroying the country. My only complaint, if Black people would only mention 'we need reparations, we need a Black Agenda' as often as mentioning Donald Trump, we might gain some traction.

Blacks call Donald Trump a racist. Let us resolve that he is. He's said some inflammatory things. In my own life to this day, I say and have said some negative things about white people. Derogatory things that could be deemed prejudicial. In short, I could be called a racist. Do I get a pass because I'm a Black nobody? Because I wasn't on national tv but in the confines of my home, in the presence of like-minded family and friends.

I don't want a pass. I spoke how I felt. Does that make me a bad person, evil? I know white people I consider friends. Does what I say in secret disqualify me from having white friends? Can I be deemed a racist and still have some good in me?

Like most Blacks where I'm from, I know there is some white in me, I'm of mixed heritage. I don't need a DNA test to know that. Some of my ancestors could pass and did pass for white on occasion. My darker skin color and nappy hair eliminated me from even trying. So all I ever knew was Black.

At the same time, I have white family members, they are in-laws. I live in a mixed neighborhood, in a city with a widely diverse population. Should I get a pass cause I don't use the 'N' word in front of my white family members and friends, cause I exercise restraint. Though I do slip on occasion in their presence.

Should I say what's really on my mind in certain situations, 'white trash,' 'trailer park trash,' 'crackers,' in front other whites? I have Black friends that use the term 'white devils', do I chastise them, no? Please, I don't want a pass. I have to do better but I will never be better if I don't cast the mirror in front of my face and see my reflection as I speak. How can we confront evil with evil and expect to change things? Race car driver Bubba Wallace had a great comeback for the attack against him by Trump, "love wins." But I know most Blacks would have had a different response.

Every time the 'N' word is shouted, Blacks turn quickly to identify who said it, why they said it. Every time a confederate flag is waved, Blacks wonder what has changed. Every time there is a lynching of a Black, Blacks realize not much has changed. What was beaten into slaves for hundreds of years can't be exorcised by not hearing words, giving a few fleeting trinkets.

The fight against racism takes a lot of energy. The sad part, we cannot legislate out prejudice and racism on both sides. More importantly, will not saying racial slurs change life on Black Man Island, a Black man's bank account, his healthcare, home address? What's in a person's heart will not change by taking down statues, renaming streets and schools.

What difference does not saying racial epithets mean, if it's in a person's heart? What is our focus? Have Blacks no power to make demands. Can't make an 'or else' statement. It would appear, that would be unamerican to the democratic party. But demands are what got Blacks this far. No one willingly cedes power. If anything, they push crumbs off the edge of the table to pacify, distract from what's needed to solve real problems.

Is our vote more important than our Black lives? Are we that insignificant? We should all ask, what difference will it make to Black folks back in the old neighborhood, on Black Man Island who the president is, what politician represents your district?

How many lives will be saved, how many jobs will be created if we can get them to stop using the 'dog whistle' words, if we stop the white nationalist from meeting, having a social media presence?

How many back in the old neighborhood really gives a damn? The politicians ribbon cut, make all the important prayer vigils and funerals, lead the monument take downs. And incredulously, we are satisfied with that?

Do most rich and powerful Black people really give a damn what goes on back in the old neighborhood? Why should they? They are living comfortably as far as they can get from Black Man Island. Why give the Black community lip service? Black America needs voices to a revolution, spoken loudly, repeatedly to the powers that be.

Powerful Blacks must tell the leaders of the Democratic Party to stop taking Blacks for granted, treating us like step-children. Treat us like we are important, to the party, this country, to the world. Give us the change we need, not what the party thinks we need. Is it too much to ask the Democratic party for anything?

Blacks are dying at an alarming rate in the streets of every democratic run city. Yet there is no national discussion to stop the killings. It's swept under the rug. No one is holding fire to the feet of politicians. No one in the media, no activists seem to want to address the problems. Why?

Donald Trump slings mud ad nauseum 24-7. His democratic detractors stay enraged. Black people are incited, mad as hell and are not willing to take it anymore. Blacks are so mad they can't see clearly. Their only wish, that the election could be today. An important question, what will happen in the Black community upon the day Trump leaves office? Will Blacks celebrate the moment and then go back to life as usual the next? <u>What is the agenda for the Black community</u>? The day after the election, what is the hope for Black America?

Oh we'll have a president that will not disparage our brothers in Africa, a president who will not detain immigrant children in detention camps. We'll have a president who will make amends with our Arab brothers. But what will a new president not named Trump mean for Black America? Black America has a laundry list of problems that fall off the page. Is there one that will be attacked upon the day the new president takes his oath of office? Where is our demand list? Where are they on the list of the Democratic Party's agenda? Give us one freebie, don't put police reform on the list.

The Black vote is our strong bargaining chips, for demanding a Black Agenda. We must not be distracted from our own babies crying, dying. We must deal with the face in the mirror, the obvious. Why are they in a position to be killed. When as Black people will we stop blaming the messenger? The question must be, why are Black men in a position to be murdered by anyone, Black or white? What can be done to change this narrative, to stop the killings from happening?

Where is the sense of boldness amongst our leaders? It's so easy to beat up the bully Trump. But can we address our friends, our allies with our needs? Who say they love us, are with us, feel our pain. Then dammit prove it.

Does it really matter who the president is? Did the needle move in the Black community, under Carter, Clinton, under President Obama's term in office? Was more food put on the table? Were more Blacks hired? Did employers suddenly decide to give Blacks a raise in honor of President Obama? The drunks are on the corner now, they were on the corner then. Did the murder rate go down under Obama? They are shooting up Chicago now, they were shooting up Chicago then and every other city where Blacks are congregated into Black Man Islands.

And guess what, you cannot blame President Obama. Seems it really does not matter who's president. The president is subject to the system, the right vs. the left. The rich have to get richer, the one percenters, the ones with all the money, who make all the rules.

Who was the last president to make the needs of Black America a priority? To date, there have been 45 American presidents. Only two administrations stand out for Black America, Abraham Lincoln's and that of John F. Kennedy/Lyndon Baines Johnson. And after Abraham Lincoln freed the slaves, it wasn't as if he kept beating the drum for the rights of ex-slaves.

Look at the list of Presidents over the last 50 years. Under which of these presidents did the needle move for Black America? One could argue that the Black community has regressed, gone back to a pseudo plantation, reconstruction era government. Blacks hold political office but wield no power.

What sticks out over the last 50 plus years, can you recall anything that jumps out for Black America, from any of the presidents?

Nixon-The Vietnam War and Watergate.

Ford-Filled Nixon's term and got the hell out.

Carter-Iran Hostage failure, inflation, high interest rates.

Reagan- "Just say no," Trickle-down economics, "Mr. Gorbachev tear down that wall."

G. H. W. Bush-Read my lips, "no new taxes" and Saddam Hussein defeat.

Clinton-The first really cool president, his welfare reform, crime bill and "I did not have sex with that woman."

G. Bush-911 and the Iraq War

Obama-Obamacare and killing Osama Bin Laden.

Trump-The Trump Tax cut, build the wall, against anything Obama.

Black America is facing real challenges that have existed for too long. Is it too much to ask the democratic party to sit down and help Black America develop and implement a Black Agenda? Is that all it takes is a few curve balls thrown our way, a few trinkets to keep us distracted? America needs no chains to hold Blacks on the island. The conditioning done through slavery keeps Blacks there, and it's perpetuated by a government that shows no spine to deal with it.

Add to that Blacks have even been sold out by our own. The white bag man walks into the rooms of the so-called Black leaders, community leaders. The Blacks are all smiles. The white man lays a suitcase full of money on the table and walks out. Guess what, the biggest fight is not about improving the community, but about how to divide up the money. These so-called leaders in turn know how to get a rise out of the Blacks, get them to the polls. Shout 'burn it down,' 'racism,' 'Nazism,' that has always worked in the past.

Blacks pay tribute to MLK's name and his accomplishments but in truth we are not very far from where he dropped us off. In many cases, you can say Blacks have gone backwards. Ask, was his dying in vain? What were our ancestors fighting for, to get us some free shit so we can sit on our ass?

THE OBAMA EFFECT

Think back to the O.J. trial of the century. Everyone was glued to their tvs. Whites were on one side, Blacks on the other side. On pins and needles, waiting on the verdict to be read. There was tension. The question, will this Black man get away with murder, was on the minds of whites? Blacks stood wondering, will a Black man catch a break for once. It'll go a long way in easing the pain of all the Black men who have dealt with the racist police and a corrupt judicial system. The verdict came in, 'Not guilty!' Whites were furious. Blacks were all smiles, celebrating as if they had won something.

Blacks knew O.J. had never done much for Blacks in the hood. But they were his staunchest supporters. Prior to the trial, if you asked him, he probably would have told you, "I'm no Black role model." Fact is many Blacks felt he was not Black. He was living the life of a Black-White man. An enviable lifestyle he did not want rocked by appearing too Black. Nevertheless, the verdict was thought a 'victory' for Black America, albeit an empty victory.

The election of President Obama went a long way in pressing the same narrative. Blacks were jubilant. Conservative whites stood there thinking, how is it that this Black man is now sitting in the white house? The white liberals gloated because they had beaten the white conservatives on the other side of the aisle. Blacks celebrated like it was December 31, 1999, when the clock struck midnight. The party was on.

The election of Barack Obama as President was, well words can't truly describe it for Black America or for whites in the deep south. For Black America, you would think the man flew in wearing a cape or road in wearing shining armor on a white horse. For

Southern Whites it like the second coming of Abraham Lincoln. If they could have assassinated him, they probably would have.

Barack Obama came to national prominence while speaking at the 2004 Democratic Convention. He was mesmerizing. As if he had outshone the headliner at a concert. He seemed to know as he spoke, it was certain nothing or anyone would or could top him. You might as well go on home. The show was over. Who else can go on? It seemed that if the Democratic Party could have, they would have run him for president that year.

His speech was destined, as if he had been practicing for just that moment. Soon thereafter, Hollywood and the Black elite jumped on board. They strategized quickly to capitalize on his talents. The phone lines lit up. He was that piece of candy everyone had to have. He became a shooting star in the Democratic Party, a man of destiny, yet no one could predict just how fast he would rise. They quickly vetted him. Admissions of trying pot, his few dalliances of romance surfaced. His beautiful family emerged, a beautiful and talented wife, two darling little girls. The prognosis, "Yep, he's our man."

Barack Obama was all in, it was beyond belief, it would appear his dreams were coming true. It seemed inevitable and so in February 2007, he announced his candidacy for president. Then the talk became, can Barack Obama really become the nation's first Black President, or will he be another Jesse? The train left the station. The 'Yes We Can' movement was born. It sounded so beautiful.

Along the way, of course he had his always Hilary detractors. They saw cracks or manufactured cracks. He should wait. He hadn't done enough in the Black community. He was just a first term Junior Senator from Illinois. Okay, so he went to Yale or was it Harvard? Shouldn't our first Black President be a Morehouse Man or some other HBCU Grad? He speaks too proper, can he relate to lower income Blacks? How will he interact with other world leaders? What does he know about foreign affairs? What does he know about economics? Afterall, he's a lawyer with no business experience. Does he have Jesse's blessing? Why won't he wait his turn? America's not ready.

His campaign theme song was, 'Your love keeps lifting me higher' by Mr. Excitement, the great Jackie Wilson. Mixed in was a chorus of, 'Yes we can." Singing of old negro hymns could be heard in churches all over the country. The world was watching. Black pride was back. His electorate was energized. On election day Blacks flocked to the polls. Record numbers of Blacks voted. Barack garnered nearly 96% of the Black vote. It was the biggest number of Blacks voting in history. He turned out record numbers of younger voters, Hispanic voters.

Upon Barack's election, seems immediately thereafter Blacks got comfortable. As if Black America had been to the mountain top and nothing else mattered. Just watching him go to sleep in the white house was enough. What more could Blacks ask or hope for? Black folk bought anything with his name or likeness on it. It was eight glorious years of don't rock the boat while Barack is in office. Blacks remained enamored with the picture, a Black man in the white house.

As the dust settled, the landscape of Black Man Islands remained unchanged. At the end of the day, Barack's last words as he left office still ring clear. Not the drop the mic moment but "Donald Trump will never be elected president of these United States." But he was. Whatever power Barack Obama held over the Black electorate was gone. Blacks stayed home, didn't worry about voting for the next president. As if all Black America's problems had been solved. So they didn't need to vote for the next president. Numbers don't lie. They tell the story. The drop in the number of Black votes was the largest percentage drop for a presidential election in our country's history.

Over the passage of time, most presidents will be remembered for the one thing, their signature legislation, a tax cut, a declaration of war, a scandal. For Barack, it will be Obamacare. Barack was motivated by his mother who fought insurance companies as she fought cancer. Obamacare was a fitting tribute if he accomplished nothing else. With politics what they are, chances are a sitting president will not accomplish a major congressional victory after his first year in office, as the partisan lines of division get drawn.

Mid-term elections alter the congressional makeup. The honeymoon is over quick.

It seemed as if after Obama became president, Blacks went off quietly back to business as usual. Seemed Blacks didn't dare ask Obama for anything, dare rock the boat, make him look bad. Blacks didn't need to see anything change for the better in Black America. Just the election of a Black man was enough. They can't take that away, that was the victory enough.

If anything, the election of Barack Obama emboldened the white southern electorate and the rust belt blue collar electorate. Combined with Black voter apathy this worked to open the door for Donald Trump. And he walked in or rode down the escalator. If anything, the election of Barack Obama divided the nation succinctly. Showed just how far America had traveled since the civil rights movement, not very far, if at all. The 2020 election is Black America's moment, a time to shift America into finishing what needs to be finished. The Black Agenda must be recognized.

THE BROWN DILEMMA

Blacks were once the country's largest minority group. Now they are in third place and fading. Blacks in America run the spectrum of color. From Black to high yellow and everything in between, from passing for white, to red, to milk-coffee, to can't even see em' in the dark. If you're a Black in America, you don't need anyone to tell you regardless of shade, you're Black American. It's a passed down legacy.

Hispanics, on the other hand are mostly sun-burned brown, with a smaller percentage who are light skinned, to maybe a small percentage who are dark skinned. But be sure, no Hispanic wants to be considered a Black American, a nigger. They watch the tv and believe everything they see on tv about Blacks, regardless of what country they come from. The perception is reality.

There was a time when we thought all folks coming from south of the border were Mexican. That was mostly the case. Today Hispanics come from enumerable countries, Mexico, Honduras, El Salvador, Guatemala, Columbia; yet they are lumped together as one, the Hispanic race. The dirty little secret no one talks about, truth is they are all different, some don't get along with each other. They don't share a similar history. There is not the common, unbreakable thread such as slavery in America, just a language.

Which brings to mind a question, why would America lump all these nationalities into one? Mexico is Mexico, Puerto Rico is Puerto Rico, Honduras is Honduras, they are all different. They are proud of their heritage. But America sees them as one. The language makes it convenient though many are born in America and can't even speak Spanish.

Where did this Hispanic thing come from? America maybe wanted to lump them in with Black Americans but that wouldn't work. White America had to do something. Voila, Hispanic was born. That's how America does it. Create another voting bloc. The only question, how strong is the Hispanic alliance? Is it a true bloc? Can a mere language do the trick?

There was a slight problem when certain Spanish speaking Europeans and South Americans decided, we're not Hispanic, we're of European ethnicity and just happen to speak Spanish. In a roundabout way, they were saying, "don't lump us in with those brown people from south of the border, the brown niggas. We're closer to white people in America." Hence, certain immigrants from Spain, South American, from Cuba refused to be lumped in with the label Hispanic, just because they speak Spanish. They were saying, we are as white as any Caucasian.

While the overwhelming majority of the Black vote here in America is connected directly to slavery, the Hispanic electorate came freely and is diverse. History tells us they will split for a variety of reasons. If a politician speaks Spanish or appeals to them directly that helps. All we have to do is look at the election of George W. Bush. A large percentage of Hispanics voted for George Bush. Then Hispanics came out strong for Barrack Obama. Hispanic voters seem listening for, 'what's in it for me.' Trump got a significant percent of the Hispanic vote. Though he stood against immigration.

Hispanics will vote differently because they want a separate alliance, maybe they have a dislike for another country. There is prejudice amongst Hispanics. All Hispanics do not want to see immigrants come across the border illegally. Countless Hispanics wait legally in line, then watch countless others cross the Rio Grande illegally and blend into the country. How does that make them feel? They watch as the numbers of illegals increase exponentially from all over. They are all after the same jobs. They know at some point the demand for those same jobs will run dry, then what.

Hispanics in America know that all immigrants crossing the border are not interested in legal activities. The last thing they want to see is the people they were trying to escape from move next door. Now there is talk afloat of open borders, ending border protection. All Hispanics are not on board. Are democratic liberals hoping that this pouring in of Hispanics will strengthen democratic election powers? That may be a stretch.

Democratic liberals appear unaware of the differences between the brown people or don't seem to care. They forge ahead as if this Hispanic Bloc is monolithic. The rally cry, 'Hispanics coming to America are fleeing war torn countries, violence, drug gangs. They want better health care, a good education, economic opportunity.' Wait, are Black communities suffering these same problems on Black Man Island? Why is there no rally cry for the needs of Black America, the Black Agenda? Appearing to pay more attention to the brown vote may cost the democratic party Black votes. They may assume too much, the overwhelming percent of the Black vote is in the bag.

THE DEMOCRATIC DILEMMA

Why pay when you can get it for free? Why buy the cow if the milk is free? What has Black America asked of the Democratic party for its continued voting loyalty? Why do our Black leaders, politicians follow the democratic party lock in step with whatever agenda they push?

Our Black elected and civic leaders are routinely coddled for the Black vote. The Black electorate is for the most part controlled by the few, like a herd of sheep. On a local level, it could be a few business leaders, a few preachers, long-time political activists, grass roots political organizations. On a state level, it could be an association of religious leaders, a group of local elected officials. On a national level it could be a group of state elected officials, the Black Caucus, a national religious association, the left leaning political pundits. Regardless, their mission appears always the same, keep the Blacks voting as a bloc.

Now when Blacks were given the power of the vote in America there was probably a natural allegiance to the Party of Lincoln. We can assume Blacks felt obliged to repay their emancipation. However, when the freed Black man began to prod for civil rights from the Republican party there was resistance. With Republicans alienating the Black vote, it became a trade-off. The so called Dixiecrats began gradually exiting the democratic party. And Blacks moved to a more liberal leaning democratic party.

When did the Democratic party completely lose the southern white male vote? June 11, 1963 on national tv, Governor George Wallace defiantly stood in the doorway of the University of

Alabama. We will not allow niggas into the University was his adamant stance. He was defiant until federal officers physically moved him aside. Until that moment Governor Wallace was the poster child for the southern democrat. Suddenly, his scowl was gone. He looked as if he had been stabbed in the back. These white people were siding with niggers. He wondered, what is happening to America? The south had lost another war.

Essentially the Governor's powers were superseded by the federal government. To him it was apparent he had been betrayed by his Democratic Party led by JFK and his brother RFK. He refused to accept that the handwriting was on the wall, the feds didn't have a choice. Integration was the law of the land. He appeared bewildered. White people were supposed to stick together against the Blacks. It was a turning point for the Democratic Party.

Vowing revenge, in 1968 Wallace ran for president as an independent. The rift was firmly established, red states vs blue states. Poor southern whites effectively left the Democratic party for the Grand Old Party, the GOP. It was an uneasy alliance. The rich Republican traditionalist of the north and the poor crackers of the south, the Dixiecrats. But It was a necessary allegiance. The GOP realized they couldn't win nationally without the infusion of southern voters and held their nose with the alliance. Then again, the Dixiecrats would not vote shoulder to shoulder with Blacks and their sympathizers under any circumstances. It's crazy. Poor whites who have more in common with poor Blacks saw no way to align with the Democratic party.

Since the signing of civil rights legislation, has there been a presidential election when Blacks have not been almost totally aligned with the Democratic party. Perhaps paying back for the passing of civil rights legislation. Apparently, that has been enough to keep Blacks at bay. However, since the passing of civil rights legislation the needle has barely moved for the Black community. We can argue infinitum about minor victories through the years, plugging holes in the dike. But it will not change the narrative of the inner city's condition.

With our Black communities struggling, can we press our white democratic friends? Can we get Black activists, Black politicians to call out the party? Would it be asking too much for them to consider prioritizing the Black Agenda?

The list of demands on the democratic leadership grows long. Immigration reform, high drug costs, LGBTQ rights, women's rights, settling Palestinian and Israeli differences, the Green New Deal are just a sampling of the list. Despite the continuing struggles in the Black community, its needs are nowhere in the picture. Black America appears unaware. Again, don't sell Black America 'police reform' is an agenda item. That's too cheap.

How long can a person be expected to continue doing the same thing and expect a different result? Black America is bringing up the rear and continues to lose ground. In the vicinity of status quo has become a comfortable place.

To manifest significant change, the Black vote must be bargained for. Relying on bleeding hearts is hit or miss. If Black America wants real change, it must stop playing nice with the democratic process. Sometimes you have to play hard. Lives must be valued, along with the vote. Ruffled feathers can be smoothed over another day.

Still there is a larger question, does Black America truly want change? Or is want of change a passing malaise? Comes and goes with the seasons. An innocent Black man gets shot down, change is badly needed. Football season rolls around and we'll take up change next year. A democrat gets in office and surely they'll take care of needed change. That's what they ran on. Change doesn't happen and Blacks are right back where they never left.

The final question, does Black America have the stomach to force change, to rock the boat of the Democratic party? You have to respect AOC, congresswoman from New York. She's young, she's brash. Her opinion, it's time old white politicians stepped aside. Even if you don't agree with Senators Bernie Sanders and Elizabeth Warren, they don't have a problem rocking the boat. If only our Black Democratic leaders were taking notes.

PART VI. HOPE TO CHANGE

WHERE DOES OUR POWER LIE?

How long is too long to wait? If you follow the politics of Black America, hope is a big word that has shown small results. Since the civil rights movement, seems Blacks have become satisfied and pacified with the minor. Let's summarize. What is the condition of Black Man Islands in America? Broken families, broken homes, fragmented neighborhoods, lack of opportunity, scarce education, Blacks preying on each other. There appears no escaping the plantation system in America. Trapped not by fear of master's beatings should they escape but trapped by an inherited conditioning of slavery.

Rather than strengthen Blacks, the politicians lead us to believe, we need dependency, we deserve more free stuff. Free is better than reparations. And so, Blacks continue to eat out of master's hands. Why change? The question must be asked. Are Black Americans fearful of not having the government's hand beneath them, holding them up?

Can Black people stop settling for handouts, allowing their problems to be covered up. In the Black community, hope is just another word for wait. It is indeed unfortunate. There is hesitancy to tie the ills of Black America to slavery. The reflection America refuses to look at, refuse to address in its totality. Until someone can explain the conditions of impoverished Black America, why should this mindset change?

The politics of the government only appears to hamper Blacks with titles such as disadvantaged, minorities, underprivileged. All that sounds like slave master talk. Put a crutch under them, 'these poor Blacks,' they can't seem to figure it out. Therefore, the consensus, we must give them charity, toss them the scraps of entitlements. Whites have always presumed, Blacks don't need reparations, for what? When they have entitlements. Even though nary an entitlement has for Blacks only.

There is a need for leadership in the Black community, be it white, Black, green, purple. Leadership willing to drive a wedge in between Blacks and free. Freedom ain't free, free ain't really free. We need out of the box leadership, willing to go against the grain. Some time ago, Bernie Sanders made a valid point. And I paraphrase, "You have to be willing to challenge and confront the norms." That's the starting point.

Do we have to crawl on our bellies, not to the folks on the right but to the liberal left. Dr Martin Luther King Jr puts this predicament into context, in his letter penned while in a Birmingham jail cell. Dr. King was in jail for protesting injustice in Birmingham. No doubt, he was tired and worn down. And what does he get, an unflattering letter from a handful of local white preachers. In essence, they scolded him. Questioning why had he come down here to agitate the fine people of Birmingham. They wanted to know, "why can't you just wait?"

Dr. King replied with a scathing letter, mind you this was in August 1963. The following is an excerpt from his letter:

"I have almost reached the regrettable conclusion that that the Negroes great stumbling block in the stride toward freedom is not the White Citizens Councillors or the Ku Klux Klanner but the white moderate who is more devoted to order than to justice; who prefers a negative peace which is the absence of tension to a positive peace which is the presence of justice; who constantly say, 'I agree with you in the goal you seek, but I can't agree with your methods of direct action'; who paternalistically feels he can set the timetable for another man's freedom; who lives by the myth of time; and who constantly advises the Negro to wait until a more convenient season".

The Democratic party and the Liberal elite might need to feel uncomfortable. What am I saying? Simply this, I fear the Republican party could offer Blacks a reparation deal and the Black politicians and pundits would shoot it down at the urging of the Democratic leadership. Before you protest, the Republicans are not going to offer reparations, but neither are the Democrats, at least not willingly. Is there any built up loyalty for the years of voting Democrats into office for Blacks? We must find out.

Where is the Black New Deal? Bottom line, are Blacks afraid to ask what's on the Democratic presidential candidate's platform for Black America? Are we on any page, at the bottom of the page? Do they know what Blacks want, need? Do they care to know?

You can find the essence of the Black man's plight in the words penned by Maya Angelou, "You may write me down in history with your bitter twisted lies, you may trod me down in the very dirt, but like dust, still I rise." Nothing has changed. She was saying, we had to fight from day one and we're still fighting. We will always be fighting. One thing is sure, you will not defeat Black people by acting as if you don't know what we're talking about.

For Blacks, there is an untold story. To take sadness, pain, anguish, the bottom of the barrel, the scraps off the table, the nothing, and 'still I rise,' will not die. Blacks were not supposed to make it but they're still here, thriving where they can, when given the opportunity. We must rise, we are the cream.

In 2020, Black America is perceived as being in last place in so many categories. One has to wonder, how is it that Blacks in America are last and behind in so many categories, and yet Blacks are leaders in countless other categories. So much so they are the envy of the world. The world wants to look like us, dress like us, act like us, dance like us, play like us, be cool like us. The world envies us but refuses to be us. How, why this contradiction?

On the plantation, the slave master's plan was to design slaves that were physically superior to work the fields. Choosing to mate the biggest buck with the plantation's slave females. This planned manipulation led to the development of Blacks with unparalleled physical superiority. Thus giving rise to Black athletes having dominated in so many sports for so many years.

After the slave's work was done in the fields and in the house, the slave master's work for them was not done. The slave master prodded slaves to entertain. Fighting, singing, dancing, acting a fool, the slave worked to please master, keep them happy. Maybe master will go easy on the plantation's slaves. Imitated and made fun of in the old minstrel shows. Forced to enter through the back door to entertain white America. Still, Blacks rose. Today Blacks are some of the world's biggest stars in the entertainment world and have been since they walked off the plantation.

Slaves were forced to survive off the scraps off master's tables. They found a way, creating a tasty meal of pig feet, pork rinds, pig ears, boudin, hog maul, blood pudding, oh yea chitlins. The scraps that turned master's stomach, wouldn't dream of eating, slaves turned into a mainstay, a delicacy, their go to survival meal. Today Black faces are on the packaging of food items, spices. Their soul food, creole cuisine is easily distinguishable in restaurants around the world. It appeared slaves had fashioned something out of nothing. They rose.

Out of the pain of their suffering, slaves evolved into a force. What the slave master meant for evil, had indeed turned into good. It only proved, when given the opportunity, Blacks can and will rise. Where does their power lie? It's in the DNA of slavery. Yet the government designs for Blacks a patchwork of entitlements, not created to overcome the problems of Black America but to keep Black America pacified, eating out of the hand of the government. What is this government fearful of?

How to Effect Change?

What needs to change? What will change look like? Let's be perfectly clear, it's not a money thing it's a numbers thing. The reality is in plain sight. The numbers don't work, will never work.

The Black population is about 13.5 percent of America's population, Black males are less than half of that. Yet Black males make up around 40% of the prison population.

The poverty rate amongst Blacks is over 20%, it's 10% for whites.

The unemployment rate for Blacks is generally double that of white America.

Blacks are denied home loans in numbers double that of whites.

Black females are the head of 72% of Black households.

Blacks lag 10 percentage points behind whites in obtaining a college degree.

Blacks typically earn around 65% of what whites earn.

Blacks life expectancy is years less than that of whites.

The list goes on and on. 150 years after slavery ended, Blacks are still in the back, bringing up the rear. Why aren't the numbers reversed or on par with white America? Some would have us believe, it's the size of a Black man's brain. Others, he's just born that way. Surely, it's an inherent trait of the Black race. *What bullshit!*

Hardly, it has more to do with who's in control. It's called oppression. When you start the 100 yard race in America, you find Blacks 50 yards back with lead boots on their feet. What are the expected results? When the majority of Blacks fail, finish last, end up in jail, we hear the narrative of old slave masters, "just dumb niggers, lazy, not good for much of anything." Wait. Where is a Black man supposed to finish in this race? If by chance a Black man gets off the plantation, 'why he's a credit to his race.' Really.

Second class is the Black's birthright, in education, housing, healthcare, in opportunities. Very few are born into opportunity. The lead boots of discrimination are still the norm. The Black man is shackled, put in the back and white America is shocked that 50% of crime is committed by Blacks. Rather quickly blame Blacks, "Blacks need to do something about the crime in their neighborhoods." White privilege is a mother.

The Numbers Must Change

Failure to address the issues affecting Black America is costing America, not saving America money. What would be the savings if a Black child was steered clear of a life of crime? What if each Black child received the best education, was given the opportunity to go to college? Lived in a safe environment, in adequate housing? If the drugs were in the hospitals and not in the streets?

What would be the production if more Blacks were at work, living productive lives, rather than being stuck in jail or unemployed? What would be the savings if more families were off the system of welfare, food stamps? But then again is that the plan, keep Blacks dumb downed eating out master's hands? Have conditions improved or gotten worse since the entitlements began to flow into Black communities? We don't need a multi-million-dollar study to ascertain the answers. Pick up the newspaper, watch some reality tv, take a walk around the Black Man Islands.

We Must Sweep In Front Our Own House

The Three Ps

Before we ask someone for their support needed to affect change, Blacks must clean up front their own house. For too long Blacks have been let down by their own. We must stop looking in all the wrong places for our salvation. We must beware the three ps. No, not pimps, pushers and prostitutes, they may even offer the most hope. Rather, I speak of our Politicians, Political Pundits and our Preachers. We can no longer wait on them to save us. The bigger question, is their heart into saving us?

Why do Blacks continue to listen to the politicians, political pundits and preachers? What are their motives? More, more, more, more money, more power, more pussy, more tv time in front tv cameras, on the tv talk shows, the evening news. They can't seem to get enough. Maybe they figure the situation is hopeless on Black Man Island, so why try.

Where is the politician who can tell anyone, in any party, if my brother is in need, I don't have a friend if they are not with me in the struggle for reparations. If my brother's house is on fire, I have to go in and save him or die trying. Who's with me? You'll find out true friends when you ask for help that requires sacrifice by the supposed friends.

The Three Ps are always politically correct. They seem to always know what's best for us Blacks. They always say what's politically correct and few if any are willing to stray from the hot topic. Are they willing to risk their job, their paper to say what needs to be said? Are they willing to call out both parties, the politicians on both sides and avow, "America should be ashamed? This American Democracy has been abusing, discounting, taking for granted the Black citizenry for too long."

Where is the needed boldness from the Three Ps, have we forgotten those who died in the struggle? We need unmitigated gall. Lest we forget how it looks, what it took. All we need do is look to a few of the forebearers of the civil rights movement. The sacrificial lambs who died in the struggle.

June 12, 1963-Medgar Evers

November 22, 1963-John F. Kennedy

February 21, 1965-Malcom X

April 4, 1968-Martin Luther King, Jr.

June 6, 1968-Robert F. Kennedy

December 4, 1969-Fred Hampton

At some point in life, a person should know what they would be willing to die for. The struggle was never about free shit. The fight was about a level playing field. The fight was about equal opportunity under the law. The fight today is about lest we forget curing the cancer gripping our inner cities. Flipping the script, reversing the numbers. This requires a revolutionary change. The prison walls of Black Man Islands must be torn down. Fred Hampton said it best, "You can jail revolutionaries but you can't jail the revolution." We will rise. We must rise.

A Bridge To Change

The one thing

Black America has to move past waiting on other people to get it, to see it. To feel our pain, they may never get it, never see it. We cannot get mad if they don't get it, see it. It may not be that they are blind. It may not be that they don't want to see, to get it. It might be like a math problem they can't solve.

Burning, looting, attacking on social media won't get them to see. Bad behavior doesn't solve problems, only clouds the situation. We have to look at the groundwork already laid by MLK. He got it. Some may have called his methods cowardice, called him an Uncle Tom. Whether it was from God or through his dreams. He knew what was needed, he had a vision.

MLK's strategy was not, just turn the other cheek. He discovered you have to find the soft tissue, where applied pressure brings about pain. The soft tissue is what matters to a people, a demographic. Could be their pride, their children, their money, could be a power struggle between left and right, could be a tax cut, a Green New Deal, immigration reform, could be women's rights, reduced medical care costs. Could be as simple as pointing a mirror in a person's direction. Everybody needs something. Black America must realize, it has the power to change things. If it doesn't faint, stays focused.

Knee jerk reaction

If we react with a knee jerk reaction, it's going to cost Black America. Major changes are generational. We must not settle for the small victory. The past would only continue to repeat, it would not be enough.

Right now, Black America is in the midst of police reform demands. But we skirt around the real problems by focusing on the symptom. We must address the, why Black men are in a position to be murdered at the hands of the police? If we only address police policy changes, we miss the boat.

If Blacks only focus on the police killings of Black men, we miss the greater problem of Black on Black murders. We must get to the root of the why. The lingering effects of slavery are mental. We are no longer in chains. The chains are around our minds. The chains grapple about our psyche. Blacks don't see a way off the Black Man Islands, so they succumb. To affect the escape from Black Man Islands for all, we must build bridges. Blacks cannot build them alone. Forging coalitions are the bridges that must be built.

<u>Who Can We Depend Upon?</u>

What about the Blacks that made it?

Can we count on the Black men and women who have done well for themselves, work hard in corporate America, maybe own their own business? What about the pro athletes, they have worked hard and have earned the big contracts? What about the entertainers, actors, the singers, the comedians, the producers now commanding the big bucks?

I know we can. First off, don't send money. I know a big sigh went up. More than money, Black America needs the voices of rich and powerful Black people. To bang the drums, sound the alarm on behalf the Black community. They have influence. They have their Twitter followers, the social media presence that reaches the masses. They have a voice with corporate America. They have strong media connections. They need only use their bully pulpit influence to help advance the causes of Black America.

What about the Black Diaspora?

Natives of Africa, Haitians, Caribbean Islanders, they migrated to this country and they observe Blacks, may think Blacks are lazy, misguided. Will they stand with us? Hell yea, they are our brothers and sisters in the struggle, they are with us.

What about the Jewish liberals?

Are they with us or are they just interested in using us? They surely don't need our money, they have more than enough. We can argue about how much was stolen from Blacks another day. Nevertheless, their Jewish Synagogues are being attacked. Anti-Semitic rhetoric is always spewed their way. Hate toward the Jewish community has been on the upswing. They need allies.

Can we count on them? They need our support and our votes to strengthen Anti-Semitic legislation. To gain our support they need to come out of the shadows and visibly support Black America's needs for reparations. If they stand for us, we must stand with them.

What about our Hispanic brothers?

If the chips were down, push came to shove. Go ask them, "are you with us?" They are good people. But based on where they came from, they might think Blacks got it made. They come from poverty stricken, war torn, gang run countries. Nothing was handed them when they got here, they had to earn it. Will they stand with us on reparations?

Let's assume the majority of Hispanics don't favor reparations. Why is that? Doesn't matter. Coalition building starts by listening to the needs of others. Focus on what they want and need. Do Hispanics need the support of Black Americans? Yes they do. Mention DACCA, immigration reform, a path to citizenship, they'll understand why. If Blacks agreed to support the Hispanic agenda on immigration, then they must support reparations for Blacks.

What about the crazy rich Asians?

Forget about it. Can you speak Chinese, Vietnamese, any ese? They are talking about Blacks as they take their money, while getting nails done, buying weave, liquor, some shrimp fried rice and chicken wings. They don't appear to want anything from Black folks but their money.

The Asian community is deep in the Black community with their restaurants, corner stores, hair product stores, nail salons. They buy real estate in Black neighborhoods and become landlords. In essence, they need Black dollars. Threaten to cut off the Black dollars and they would quickly get the picture and gladly support reparations.

What about the Arabic brothers?

They are entrenched in the Black community. Blacks visit their stores and businesses daily. What's their conversation about? Are they interested in anything Blacks have to say? Check out their prices. What's the mark up like? That says a lot. Will they stand with us?

Arabs are seeking fair treatment from the government. Ever since 911, they are looked upon as problematic in our society. Can we trust them? What are they up to? Their mosques have come under close scrutiny, even assault. Their entry into the country is limited and scrutinized. They would appreciate the support of the Black community, we are brothers. Well we would appreciate and must have their support for reparations, whether they believe we should have them or not. They understand well, quid pro quo, they will give their support.

The Art of Coalition Building

The new math

We must build voting coalitions, starting with non-whites to effect elections. What do we have in common? The commonality, none of the aforementioned, regardless their skin tone will ever be considered white. Regardless their hair texture, income, the titles in front and behind their name, where they hail from, where they live, who they live next to, nor who they know, matters not. We are all looked upon as non-white, that's where we start to build our coalition.

The old white electorate is dying off, fading away. The white electorate is shifting. A more liberal leaning white electorate is emerging. White women are breaking free of their husbands voting penchants. White soccer moms are concerned about women's rights, their children's health, their education, maternity leave, equal pay. What about the LGBTQ community? They are concerned about discrimination and violence. What about the far left of the Democratic party, that wants a green economy? We must join forces, we share most their needs.

What about poor whites? Their struggles are just as real. They need us and don't even realize it. They must wake up. We have more in common than we have differences.

These demographic splinters must be marshalled into one force. Once we have a coalition, we will have a voice that cannot be denied. We will be given a seat at the table. Then again, what happened to civility in American politics? It's so polarized. Politicians act as if they can't reach across the aisle to the other party? They must decide, are our differences and disagreements more important than our value and love for this country?

The Black community must recognize voting is the thing. If we all want change, it has to be about power and control over elections. Elections have consequences. Our goal must be to build and maintain coalitions.

We must press our brothers and sisters as if their lives depended on the outcomes of elections, the young and old must register to vote. If a Black is not registered to vote they trample upon their ancestors who died for their right to vote. If Blacks don't vote they trample upon their children's lives. Expecting things to change for the better on their own is a pipe dream. We must vote like Obama is on the ballot every election.

The good news, voting is painless. It's liberating. You can even get a free ride to the poll. As of late, you can even request a mail-in ballot. Can you imagine the fear in this country if Blacks voted in the 90 percentile range for all elections? That's a scary thought.

A Black Agenda

The Decision

Estimates for reparations are all over the place. Some estimates suggest sixteen trillion, some fifty trillion. Black America has to make a decision. What are we really fighting for? Do we want a reparations check or lasting change? Do we want permanent change or ephemeral change? A reparations check would put money in a Black family's pockets for a while and then it's gone. Giving them fleeting enjoyment, maybe?

Cash payments will not solve the problems of Black America deeply rooted in a slavery system. If anything, they may create more. We all have seen too many brothers receive a cash settlement, in the six figures, seven figures and go through the money in a heartbeat, end up homeless or worse, dead. Brothers with no business knowledge will open up businesses, fund their friends, party like never before. In the end, lose all their settlement.

Sisters get their settlement money and their man is first with his hand out. Won't settle for a basic car or truck, has to have the top of the line. Will wreck it and want another. Go through his woman's money and have no idea where it went. After it's all gone, sisters will look for another line to get in.

I know and understand the temptation. Most Blacks would love a check, but we must look beyond cash. A cash payment in and of itself will not permanently lift all boats. What do I mean? In short, every Black person is not equipped to handle a large sum of money. Particularly Blacks on Black Man Island who have little or no financial expertise. We must not be derailed by a focus on a check.

Money presents problems. How do we equate a dollar in small towns with that of a dollar spent in the big and expensive cities? Dumping money into the Black community's hands would bring about the worst in people. The worst characters would find their way to Black Man Islands to con and pillage.

Black America needs surgery. Surgery represents permanent change, a lasting change for our children's children future. Permanent change is not a band aid, won't just dress up problems. Permanent change is required to overcome the DNA of the slavery system, perpetrated on Black America. Permanent change is the purpose of a revolution.

In 2020 whether Black America is aware or not, The Democratic Party is moving to appease the far left of the party, they have a voice and an agenda. Figuratively speaking, The Green New Deal is on the ballot. Costs to implement the Green New Deal are estimated at 50 to 90 trillion dollars over ten years. Immigration reform, open borders, ICE dismantling is on the ballot whether Blacks realize it or not. Bernie Sanders wants free healthcare and free college tuition for all. His voice will have to be heard. The LGBTQ community is demanding their equal rights, they will have to be heard.

America will be voting for or against all the above and more. All that is good. However, the underlying question for Black America, where is the 'Black New Deal?' Black America cannot sit back and anticipate their problems being taken care of by anybody. Black America must create its Black Agenda.

What is a Black Agenda?

The Black Agenda is the listing of problems intrinsic to the Black community and the solutions to those problems. The Black Agenda is problem specific. The Black Agenda is about major surgery not band aids. What is surgery? Boldness to say, if it's not working, be prepared to throw it out. If it's not working, hasn't been working, why continue the insanity.

A Starting Point-A Six Point Plan

1. Reform Education First

We must rethink education in the public school system. We must get education right. Education is key to tearing down walls. Education frees the mind, takes the shackles off. America must stop the culture of funding failure where education in the inner city is concerned. We keep trying to fit Black kids in a box. They are unique individuals with different needs. They have problems that are unique to their circumstances, their environment.

If the Black Agenda accomplishes nothing else, it must reform the education system of Black America. The critical question, why do we send our kids to schools that don't work? We must be prepared to throw out schools as we know them. Period.

We must not allow Black children to fall behind in a class and never catchup. Label them, give up on them early and later wonder what happened? Send them on to the next class ill prepared. Before we spend another dime on a broken system of education in the Black community, we must research and correct the why they are failing.

Some suggestions

Can we modify the behavior of the Black youth in America? Get our children to dream big, look beyond what they see in their community, their plantation environment. Look beyond sports and entertainment, selling drugs, getting on welfare as the only ways out.

Why can't we have smaller public school classrooms? Today, a teacher must be more than an instructor. They must spend adequate time with each pupil. We are quick to argue the cost of smaller education classes is too expensive. But we are quick to fund incarceration, new and larger jails, more judges, more police, more money for the public defender's budget, the DA's budget. That's backwards thinking, that's funding an expected failure.

The public system of education is entrenched in our culture but why do we need cookie-cutter public schools. We should be prepared to throw out curriculums as we know them. That are not working anyway. If need be, kill the concept of the public school system as we know it. In the urban setting, most public schools are failing anyway. And because of that, most of our kids are failing in life.

Why do we need teachers who ascribe a child's potential before they know the child? Based on how they look, how they dress, how they talk, the neighborhood's they are from. Why can't we select the best teachers, creative teachers for our public schools? Why can't we pay our public school teachers at these so-called difficult and failing schools above that of the best schools? Incentivize their pay, give them bonuses for results.

What is being taught in school? Is there artificial intelligence education in our schools, business entrepreneurship, money management? The new curriculum must include more than reading, writing and arithmetic. Where are the basic life skills in the curriculum?

Are the new economy skills being taught? Why not invest in emerging technologies for public schools? Why not seek to build the best mousetrap and let others beat a path to the door of those schools? Play the Steve Jobs tape, inspire imagination, innovation. Why can't there be a Black Bill Gates or Steve Jobs in our community, if given the right opportunity? How many Black students are exposed to Black technology icons? Believe technology opportunities are within their reach?

Why can't we create new schools designed to find a child's gift? Why not forget about grade advancement. All children are not ready to fly off at a given time. Let them graduate when they are ready to fly. If they don't succeed at one school, let them try another. Let us not penalize a child for being different.

Is becoming successful mentioned in class? Is encouragement offered daily? What about the pursuit of gainful employment, a career? Is how to fill out a job application, prepare for an interview in the student's curriculum? What about how to dress for an interview? How to field interview questions? How to survive in this crazy world? Are these skills requisite to graduation?

Why can't we dedicate a percentage of the student's day to life concerns. We don't hear enough, 'I am somebody,' anymore. Why can't that be a daily anthem, part of the daily curriculum? Mentoring is a cornerstone to a child's stability and growth. Why can't we ensure that every boy has a father figure in his life. Every girl has a mother figure. Mentors can teach children about anger management, how to overcome peer pressure, help build character. Every school should be required to find out, does a child have meaningful and reputable parental figures in the home. The community must be the safety net to prevent children being lost.

2. Strengthen The Black Family

Children are the future. They matter. The Black agenda must fund programs to ensure children have a safe place to lay their head, receive a wholesome meal and adequate clothing. Even more so, they must be provided the nurturing and encouragement of home life.

How do we solidify and strengthen the splintered Black family? We must first acknowledge and understand what we're dealing with. Over 70% of families in the Black community are headed by a single female. Many Black children are orphaned, abandoned, living with surrogate family members, a grandmother, aunts, living from pillar to post. Where, what is our safety net for these families and kids? A Black Agenda may not save all of Black adults in need, but we must 'save the children.'

3. Jobs & Economics

A Black agenda must put more money into the pockets of lower income Black Americans. Nothing makes an adult feel good inside like having money in their pocket, to pay bills, treat the family to a nice meal, take a vacation, splurge on the kids. A Black agenda must work to have minimum wages raised without delay. Additionally, Black America needs real jobs for financial growth, not a plethora of minimum wage jobs. Corporate America must be pressured to relocate and build offices and plants in the Black Community.

Corporate America must work to employ youth through apprenticeships in lieu of forthcoming jobs. On the job training should be widespread in high school, not the exception. We must face the new reality about jobs in the Black community. Certain jobs are gone and are not coming back. We must focus on training for the new economy's jobs and needs. Businesses must partner with high schools, vo tech schools, so that they are made aware of their employment needs.

Starting new Black owned businesses is imperative to rebuilding communities. New business developments must be advocated for in the Black community. A Black agenda must bring back the small Black businesses. Creativity and entrepreneurship must be encouraged in school and in the community with adequate funding readily available. A Black agenda must provide entrepreneurship training in the community, backed by grants and low interest loans. Aspiring new business owners must not be sidetracked by prioritizing credit and income qualifications by lenders in the lending process.

<u>4. Police & Justice Reform</u>

Why is this so difficult, taken so long? The Black agenda must require police departments serving the Black community to change. We must have confidence in our police to do what is right. Serve the community, work within the community not just in the community.

Police must be required to undergo thorough training in the community before they work the community. A Black agenda must require the Black community have a say in the restructuring of police departments that serve the Black community.

Why are we locking up Black men at alarming rates in this country? There is talk of defunding the police, the Black agenda must work to defund the prison system. Non-violent offenders should not be locked up, rather we must work to place them in diversion programs funded by prison defunding.

5. Rebuilding the Infrastructure of the Black Community

Home ownership must be encouraged and made affordable. Home ownership is the backbone of the community. The government spends more money to house a poor family than it costs to build a house and give it to a poor family. This has to change.

Healthcare must be made readily available and affordable in the Black community. Healthcare must encompass prevention and not just care. Drug companies should be defunded to help fund comprehensive healthcare in the Black community.

Predatory lending must be eliminated in the Black community. Caps must be placed on interest rates charged by unscrupulous lenders. Community lending must be developed in the Black community.

A revolution can start by making small steps. Funds should be provided for youth cleanup programs. Clean up the litter on neighborhood streets, whitewash graffiti. Provide funds to remove or repurpose blighted structures. Perception of change becomes reality.

6. Political Accountability

Why don't we vet our politicians? Ask them, why should I vote for you when I don't know you? We elect politicians but our responsibility should not stop there. We more importantly must hold them accountable. We must require report cards on their time in office. If they fail to deliver, receive a failing grade, then they should not even run for reelection. A Black agenda should include a push towards the federally funding of all political campaigns.

The 'Black New Deal'

Create an Acronym for the needed legislation. Call the Black Agenda *The 'TEAR ACT,' (The Education And Reform Act)*, The 'BEAR ACT,' *Black Education And Reform Act. Doesn't have to be called Black anything, call it, 'Urban Revitalization Program,' 'Urban Renewal Act'* or whatever. Regardless of the name, a Black Agenda must be part of the Democratic Party's agenda.

We must establish a budget for the Black Agenda, if it's not in the trillions, that's a non-starter. That's not saying it has to be 16 trillion, it could be 5 trillion, 10 trillion, 2.3 trillion. It just has to have a 'T' in the amount for starters.

In 2019 we started out with over 20 candidates for the Democratic nomination. And it was like they were playing a game of gotcha. Did it matter that they were just trying to say what we wanted to hear, without stepping on a politically incorrect landmine? Can we face reality and accept the fact that they can't and won't deliver on few if any promises? We set our aim high and settle for the nothing they deliver on. Then reelect them as they pass on blame.

The election is coming, one is always coming. How do you determine if someone is with you? You have to ask them for something. The lip service is all well and good. But when you are in desperate need, will they come through? We must ask, will the Black Agenda be put on the party's agenda? The Democratic Party needs our vote, there has never been a more important election. We must have a Black Agenda. The Democratic Party has already counted the Black vote. According to Joe, "you ain't Black if you don't vote for me." They may have our votes counted but they must not be allowed to ignore our need for a Black Agenda.

It seems for too long Black America has valued acceptance more than needs. It appears we don't want to be seen as party crashers. But our blood is flowing in the streets. Our mothers are crying tears of sadness. Our men are being stacked in prisons. Major surgery is needed and America keeps applying partial payments and band aids of entitlements to the patients.

For too long, we look to the government to solve all our problems on Black Man Island. Creating this perceived need of must have. Blacks must understand, for the most part, when in control, the government does not solve problems, it creates problems. Many of our ills are the result of some ill-advised or antiquated government rule or law. Why do we chase ghosts? We must decide what's best.

Let us stich this together. Run a needle and thread through this. Every metropolitan area, large and small with a significant Black population is suffering the same problems, same ills. The politcos say it's a Black problem. For sure, it's not the Black on us, it's the slavery in us and the failure of America to right the wrongs of slavery and mistreatment of Blacks for the past 150 plus years.

THE CLOSING ARGUMENT

Funding a Reparations Bill:

Why did the government deny ex-slaves reparations upon setting them free? We know for sure, Black Lives did not matter in 1865. No one was speaking for Blacks. There was no representation, no NAACP, no Urban League. They couldn't make demands of anyone for anything. They in a word were stuck, between a rock and a hard place. So this brings us to today, we speak for the long since dead and the living, why to this day have there been no reparations America?

Objection number 1, It will cost too much.

The Government might suggest, look at the costs of the civil war to the country. Can that amount be subtracted, a lot was spent, a lot of lives lost?

The defendants reply, the Civil War was a terrible and costly war but what does the Civil War have to do with reparations?

The Government counters, with all the recent disasters, wars, the pandemic, America simply can't afford a reparations bill.

The defendants respond, does justice in America have a price tag? Is there a monetary cutoff point? Reach a dollar amount and cancel out any judgement. If so, then that's not justice. Put a price tag on what's needed to solve the problems created by slavery in America, be it a trillion dollars or ten trillion, whatever. If anyone questions the money, start with a fair price tag on the free labor done by slaves. Put a price tag on unfair labor practices, the beatings, the lynching, the rapes. Put a price tag on all that has been stolen from Blacks, in cash, intellectual property, inventions, culinary recipes, music, land. Put a price on all the decades of injustice, discrimination done to Blacks. Of course, add to costs, with interest and penalty.

The Government counters, this is going to bankrupt America.

The defendants respond, America sent checks to just about every adult in America for Coronavirus stimulus support. Some of the adults were dead. Was there any hesitancy by the president, by congress, any thought of bankruptcy? Debt has never been a problem in America when deemed necessary. Why not refinance the debt, sell some bonds, get on a payment plan? Liquidate some assets. Borrow the money from China.

America prints money with little regard, when it's convenient. Just look at our national debt. Study the bills, they are littered with bacon for the folks back home, folks overseas, friends as well as enemies. No, costing too much is just a lame, kick the can down the road excuse, in hopes the plaintiffs die off or forget about it.

Objection number 2, The passage of time.

The Governments ask, why now? This slavery thing was so long ago. Most states were not yet in the union. Who is really to blame? Everyone associated with slavery has long since died off. Afterall the slaves were freed. Doesn't that count as enough?

The defendants respond, why wasn't the government dealt with reparations in prior years, in 1905, 1955, 2005? The government has had ample time? It appears the government does not want to do anything close to reparations, not then, not now.

Does time cancel out injustice? Does time erase what happened? Does time absolve perpetrators of injustice? If that be the case, why is there no time limitation for murder cases? Justice postponed is not justice. The light shines brighter on that injustice. We ask, why has the government avoided resolving this case for so long.

Why is time put into the equation for reparations? Is it a matter of convenience to deprive our ancestors their due? Passage of time appears nothing but a convenient excuse. Justice must be served, if not now when?

Objection number 3, The country has done enough for Blacks.

The Government suggests, hasn't America done enough for Black people? The country has already done too much for Black America. 'The country has given them civil rights legislation, affirmative action.' 'They get most all the free stuff.' 'They don't want to work.' 'This is just another attempt to get money out of the government.'

The Slaves respond, when Lyndon Baines Johnson signed the civil rights legislation, from the look on his face it did not appear he signed because he liked Black people. He looked as if someone was at his back with a gun to his head. America is quick to boast of the constitution. "We hold these truths to be self-evident, that all men are created equal." But for too long a time, justice and equality have been ignored rights for Blacks. You would think the Red Sea was parted upon the passing of civil rights legislation. All that remained was for Blacks to walk across, over to America's promise land. Instead the struggles for most Blacks continued.

Seems everything the government does has been about not giving what is needed but what the government thinks is needed. America quickly points to entitlements, what the government thinks is needed. Then turns around and blames Blacks for the failures of these entitlement programs. If anything, the little America has done has made things worse in the Black community. Shortchanging the Black community is not doing enough for the Black community. Rather shortchanging is nothing more than insulting the Black community.

Objection number 4, These things take time, years to develop.

The Government suggests, you can't solve all of Black America's problems overnight?

The Slaves respond, President Obama was elected on healthcare and he passed a comprehensive healthcare bill in just over a year of taking office. Donald Trump ran on a tax reform. Donald Trump took office January 20, 2017. Trump's tax reforms were signed into law December 22, 2017. Where there is will, America makes a way.

Objection number 5. It's not a slavery thing, it's a Black thing.

The Government suggests, every time something goes awry in Black America, Blacks come to the government wanting a bailout.

The Slaves respond, are those in America that are against slavery reparations qualified to object? Can America look at the condition of the patients? Can America examine the symptoms of the patients? Can America stop with the misdiagnosing of the patients? Can America stop applying band aids to the patient? Can America stop lying to the patient? Is it not possible that all Blacks are different? Some are not that strong. Can't just overcome obvious obstacles, roadblocks.

Some in America ask, why can't all Blacks emulate the heroes of Black History month? Isn't that why they wanted a Black History Month? Of course, that is the partial intent of celebrating, giving Blacks stars to aim for. Unfortunately, while all men are created equal in most ways, we are not all endowed with the same gifts. All Blacks are not blessed with undeniable talent and beauty. Detractors in America miss the boat. We are all endowed by the creator with certain inalienable rights, life, liberty and the pursuit of happiness, but not undeniable gifts.

Everybody can't get the medal for heroism. It's always easy from the "Other Side." But have you ever been on the other side, walked in the other person's shoes? What if whites were all Black? What if their paperwork read failed, failed or denied, denied. Can't buy because of bad credit. Can't rent because you don't look right. Can't get a job because of subjective qualifications. Can't get a decent education. All Blacks are shod with iron on their soles at birth, then reinforced and instilled with negativity as they grow and mature in a prejudicial environment. That's the Black's heritage in America.

Where are Blacks expected to finish in the race? They start out behind the start line. Most given little or no help, no encouragement to excel, to try harder, do better. The question begs an answer. With just a little of the proper help, how far could they have gone? A white man and a Black man born the same day to single mothers, in the same block in the hood, both drop out of the failing school system. Who do you put your money on to come out ahead? Why?

In Summary

Can a patient be allowed to tell a doctor their symptoms or is the patient going to be told how he's supposed to feel? Can how Black people feel finally be addressed in earnest? Or are we going to continue to allow white America to tell Blacks, 'there's nothing wrong with you.' As if they know what Blacks feel, what it's like to be Black. Can the behavioral remnants of slavery be inherited, passed down to heirs? Can the remnants not affect the psyche of the heirs?

Slavery happened. The United States of America did willingly allow the kidnapping and enslavement of people from the African Continent. Brought to the United States and listed as chattel, personal property. The slaves were given no rights, no pay, no regard to treatment, no recourse for inhumane treatment. No recourse for slaves beaten and lynched. No recourse for slave women raped and often impregnated by slave owners. Despite these children born to free white men they were given no rights and thusly treated as slaves. Children were taken from mothers with no regard. Sold off with no regards for a mother's rights.

Even after slavery ended the mistreatment of Blacks continued. They mostly were given a sharecropper's status, third rate jobs. Working in another form of slavery. The Jim Crow laws came into existence to keep Blacks down, segregated. Blacks continued to be discriminated against despite their freedom. Even after Jim Crow laws were outlawed, the discrimination of Blacks continued. Discrimination exists to this day.

Was the end of slavery ever about righting a wrong? If so, why no reparations? That does not make sense. Even in Biblical times, a party doing damage to another had to repay for damages, equal to the value of the damage. Even the Hebrew slaves after 400 years of bondage were allowed to take the best from their Egyptian captors.

It appears as if it has always been more important for this nation to not give the ex-slaves and their heirs too much. Give them just enough. Giving the appearance, there has to be this separation of races, keep Blacks in an oppressive state, 3/5s of a white man. White America has to have someone to step on or over, a need for a lower class, an oppressed class. Maybe not always consciously but appearances tell the story.

The Precedents

The premise of reparations is not new. The premise of reparations is to make a wrong right or attempt to make a blatant wrong right through some form of payment, a reparation. What is more worthy than reparations for slavery? All the civil rights legislation, all the well wishes did not right the ship of slavery. There is a crying out that is signaled by the blood running in the streets. The shrieking wails of mothers losing their children. Are we listening America to the scrapes across blackboards? Or does America seal its ears, look with jaded eyes as if it's but a gruesome train wreck on a reality tv program. How long are we going to ignore the glaring problems? Act as if we're too busy right now to take this up. We don't need another investigation into another investigation, all while the blood runs into our sewers. Is our blood spilt for naught?

The sexual predators

We act as if there is no precedent for reparations. At the same time, we can go back 50 years or more to resolve other wrongs. A half a century old sexual scandal in the boy scouts, thousands of boys harmed by sexual predators, what will that cost? Sexual predator Priests hiding in plain sight for decades. Pedophiles preying on young boys. The Catholic church has paid out over a billion dollars to settle cases. Rich and powerful sex offenders are going to jail and paying out millions.

The Native Americans

Native Americans were robbed and killed for the native land they occupied. Through the years congress has allocated billions in reparations. Native Americans were given the right to open casinos on Indian land. Indian tribes were given a Sovereignty status, allowing them to govern themselves and avoid state taxes. And it's not enough, more should be done.

The Internment of Japanese Americans

The Japanese in America during WWII were herded into internment camps by a fearful government. It lasted a few years. In the end the Japanese victims and their descendants got $20,000 each.

Jews

Maybe America can learn from the reparations paid by Germany to the Jewish People after WWII. Hitler killed millions of Jews and enslaved millions. The German government paid the equivalent of billions to the country of Israel and the World Jewish Congress.

Reparations, a Right and Not a Privilege

The shoulders of America's blind justice have strained to hold the load of injustice done to Blacks in America. And yet when a Black man asks the government to right the injustice, it's a problem. It's time this case gets settled. Are we who we say we are, a nation of caring people? Ready and willing to come to the aid of a people in distress wherever. Sweep in front your own house America.

Decide America, was there a transgression done by this nation to allow the enslavement of Africans and ensuing mistreatment of these slaves? Was there continued abuse done to Blacks after slavery ended? Does abuse against Blacks not continue even to this day? This nation must no longer avoid paying reparations for slavery and discount the lingering effects of slavery on Black America.

America has done nothing more than throw alcohol and band aids on the problems that persist in Black America. Ask the medical professionals. How long can the effects of slavery last? Did they automatically end with the outlawing of slavery? Look into the mirror America. The flip side of the coin is all the proof needed. Racism against Blacks is alive and thriving in America, 'inherited' by whites from their ancestors, a symptom of white privilege. White kids are not born racist. Black America has grown weary. Weary of the patronizing, every so often thrown a bone, distractions. Blacks need the justice of reparations and they need them now.

If America doesn't acknowledge the need for reparations for Blacks, then America denies slavery was wrong.

If America denies reparations for Blacks, then it denies the lynching of Blacks, the rapes of Blacks, the theft from Blacks ever occurred.

If America denies reparations, then it denies Jim Crow existed and that discrimination against Blacks does not continue today.

If America denies reparations, then is America, America?

The Unspecified Damages

There is a starting point. Can America answer what happened to forty acres and a mule? There was an agreement. This nation reneged on the apparent deal for reparations of 400,000 acres. What would have happened if the government had fulfilled the promise? What would be the value of those reparations in today's dollars? What would be the value of the estimated 400,000 acres had they been given to former slaves? What would be the total wealth of Black America today? Would all the numbers be reversed? Would Blacks continue to bring up the rear in all the right categories or would they be first?

In 1866 the federal government began the Homestead Acts, which allowed applicants rights to government land. Applicants were given from 320 to 640 acre sections of land to settle on. All told, 160 million acres of government land was effectively given away to promote growth. But the federal government couldn't give ex slaves a measly 40 acres and a mule. At the end of slavery, approximately 3.9 million slaves were freed. So what are we talking about? 400,000 acres divided by 3.9 million ex slaves. That has to be a joke but they reneged on the joke.

Convenient Injustice

Justice was certainly blind in 1865. Is justice still blind in America? Why is it so hard to settle this matter? Is justice supposed to right all wrongs or just for the select few? There has to be a way to level the playing field for delayed justice. The current state of inner city Black America is undeniable. Look to the future of Black America without reparations. Is a 'change gon' come' on the horizon, over the rainbow for Black America?

The government writes checks with countless zeros on them all the time. But the *unspecified damage* is not in checks to individual bank accounts but this case must fund the structure of a Black Agenda. We need to raise all boats of the long-suffering communities of Black America.

What is Our Affliction?

Our affliction is not our addiction. It's not the crutch we use to stand, to lean on, prop us up. All the guns, the drugs, inadequate housing, lack of proper education are symptoms, different parts of the same addiction. America, our affliction is in our slavery DNA. America, don't just watch Blacks die, give us the cure for this cancer.

www.ingramcontent.com/pod-product-compliance
Lightning Source LLC
Chambersburg PA
CBHW031331060726
47590CB00007B/2423